CW00920027

ADDINGHAM
FROM BRIGANTES TO BYPASS

John & William Cunliffe hunting with West Hall (Nesfield) and Beamsley Beacon in the background. *J. Thompson-Ashby.*

ADDINGHAM

from Brigantes
to bypass

A History

KATE MASON

PUBLISHED BY
ADDINGHAM CIVIC SOCITY

First published in 1996
Reprinted with amendments 2007
by Addingham Civic Society
5 Springfield Mount
Addingham
LS29 0JB

ISBN: 987 0 9555236 0 1

Front cover: Addingham Main Street before the railway. *Holmes Collection.*

Designed printed and bound by
SMITH SETTLE
Gateway Drive, Yeadon, West Yorkshire LS19 7XY

Contents

Preface and Acknowledgements

THIS is not a book of reminiscences. As an 'off-comed 'un' (albeit of fifty years residence) I do not feel qualified to write about Addingham in that way even though Tom Mason, my husband, was full of memories of his early life.

I have endeavoured to put the history of the village in context, to pick out interesting facts and to show what happened at different periods. I have been fortunate in having many friends who have helped and encouraged me. I cannot acknowledge them all but Mr. Alister Wilkinson of Highfield Farm, now the Lord of the Manor of Addingham, has allowed me to see all his manorial papers. Many other people have lent me deeds and photographs and spent time in discussing details with me.

Mr. S. Moorhouse surveyed the iron working site at Smithy Hill, published here for the first time. Messrs. N. and L. Wallbank allowed access on to their land to carry out the survey. Dr. R. Spence drew my attention to the 1585 map and I gratefully acknowledge the permission of the Chatsworth Settlement Trustees to reproduce it. The Bodleian Library, Oxford, holds the copyright to Nathaniel Johnstone's manuscripts and English Heritage the plan of old Lumb Beck. The picture of the old rectory is at the Borthwick Institute for Historical Research, York. Professor R. Bailey of Newcastle and Mark Whyman of the York Archaeological Trust have given me interpretations of the Viking Age cross.

Above all I have drawn mainly on papers belonging to Addingham Parish Council and St. Peter's Church. Both collections are now at the Bradford branch of the West Yorkshire Joint Archive Service. Other documents are at the Yorkshire Archaeological Society, Leeds and the Leeds branch of the West Yorkshire Joint Archive Service. I am very grateful to all the archivists for their help. The assistance of the West Yorkshire Archaeology Service in map preparation is gratefully acknowledged as is the grant towards their preparation given by the Yorkshire Archaeological Society. Idiosyncracies in spelling are quoted from the original documents.

I have had constant encouragement from Arnold Pacey and Malcolm Birdsall and also from Addingham Civic Society who are publishers of the book but all errors and omissions are my own.

Kate Mason
Addingham 1995

List of abbreviations

YAS   Yorkshire Archaeological Society
YAJ   *Yorkshire Archaeological Journal*
YASR   *Yorkshire Archaeological Society Record Series*
PRO   Public Records Office
WYJAS   West Yorkshire Joint Archive Service
BA   *Bradford Antiquary*
WYAS   West Yorkshire Archaeology Service

'Whoever was uprooting a thistle, or bramble, or draining out a bog, or building himself a house, that man was writing the history of England …'
– Thomas Carlyle in Lectures on the History of Literature 1830.

Chapter 1

The Beginnings of the Village

Before there was a village: the archaeological evidence

TODAY the traffic flows constantly through the Aire Gap along the A59 and A65 roads. These roads make the easiest east-west crossing of the Pennines following the ice-worn valleys through which the rivers Ribble, Aire and Wharfe flow within a few miles of each other. Addingham lies between the River Wharfe and Rombald's Moor where the river takes a sharp turn running north to south before resuming a more easterly course again.

Stand on the west end of Otley Chevin on a clear day and look westwards along the length of the escarpment of Rombald's Moor and Addingham Edge. The eye is led to a gap in the hills and clearly seen in this gap are the peaks of Sharphaw and Roughaw beyond Skipton, natural guides and signposts for earlier travellers. There is an easy and natural route the whole way from the North Sea right through to the Ribble Estuary and the Irish Sea. Eric Cowling (1946) called this 'Rombald's Way'. There is no evidence of a made prehistoric track but the flint for the implements of Mesolithic, Neolithic and Bronze Age men which are scattered over Rombald's Moor from Green Crag Slack to Shepherd's Hill must have been carried along this route. The tiny flints of Mesolithic hunters have been found both on the moor and by the River Wharfe at Farfield, as also flint implements of the Neolithic and Bronze Ages, but no traces of habitations or settlements from these periods.

On Rombald's Moor is a large number of carved rocks of a type known as 'cup and ring'. These rocks may have hollow carvings, reminiscent of cups, some of which are encircled by rings; other marks may also be found. They occur mainly on the north-east end of the moor on Green Crag Slack, on Baildon Moor and near Morton. Two large rocks on Addingham Moor also have these carvings on them. The significance of the carvings is unknown but a survey was carried out by the Ilkley Archaeology Group (1986). They are thought to have been made in the Late Neolithic or Early Bronze Ages.

The pollen from trees, grasses, crops and weeds was shed on to the surrounding

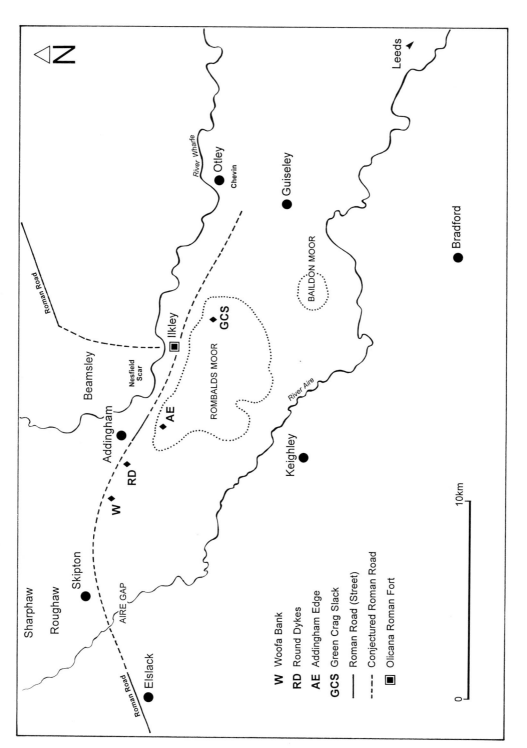

Addingham & its surroundings showing some prehistoric features. It was in the Pennines that the Brigantes mainly dwelt. Drawn by WYAS

land. This pollen was preserved in the acid peat deposits. Samples of peat taken from the moor and Seamer Tarn show a decrease in tree pollen as far back as the Neolithic period about 4000 years ago with less tree pollen in the succeeding Bronze Age as more woodland was cleared. Grass pollen and some cereal pollen suggest pasture together with a small area of arable land. The major tree clearance took place in the Iron Age, perhaps from 700BC onwards, probably because people were moving from the uplands towards the valleys.

The Iron Age people (including the Brigantes) ground their corn in coarse gritstone hand querns shaped like small straw beehives, hence called beehive querns. A sufficient number of these have been found on Addingham Moorside to suggest there might have been a settlement there though no site has been found. There is, however, an Iron Age earthwork on Addingham Low Moor. This, known as 'Round Dikes', is a circular 'camp' surrounded by a bank and ditch. Inside is an earlier Bronze Age barrow and, in the perimeter of the circle, there was, until recently, a perennial spring which did not even dry up in the long drought of 1976. More recent drainage work on the moor beyond seems to have affected its permanence.

Beyond Round Dikes and under Woofa Bank on Silsden Moor there is a very similar enclosure, and this, together with Round Dikes, is surrounded by one low earthen bank called by the Ordnance Survey 'line of circumvallation'. Round Dikes has not been disturbed or excavated but the Woofa Bank enclosure was described by Whitaker(1878) as having 'numerous rude hearths constructed of stone and filled with ashes' so that we can assume that both were groups of dwellings, perhaps protected from wild beasts, surrounded by dead hedges or wattle fences.

Across the River Wharfe, on the scar at Nesfield, is a third earthwork on a hillock or rocky eminence overlooking the river. The outline of an irregular enclosure with low banks can be seen enclosing an area of perhaps half an acre. This, together with Round Dikes and the one near Woofa Bank were supposed by Whitaker to be summer encampments of the Romans. This explanation is no longer thought to be correct. The three earthworks are each very irregular in outline as opposed to the well laid out rectangular works of the Romans. The greatest influence of the Romans was due to their fort at Ilkley with associated roads from Tadcaster through Ilkley and Addingham to Ribchester, still using the route through the Aire Gap.

The 350 year occupation by the Romans may have altered our landscape but, if so, we have not learned to interpret it. Only the Roman road, still known as 'The Street', has remained in use as a cartway and footpath. The period after the Romans left the country is truly 'dark'. Written records are sparse and for this part of Yorkshire non-existent. The archaeological record is equally blank. It was the first time that the Celtic tribe of the Brigantes lived in this part of the Pennines.

There were two shadowy Celtic kingdoms. The first called Elmet is believed to be land between the Aire and the Wharfe. Possibly there was another Celtic kingdom based on the district we know as Craven. This is a Celtic name meaning 'the land of wild garlic'. The Anglo-Saxons (in Yorkshire the Anglians) attacked and defeated the men of Elmet in 612 AD and also started to occupy the Lancashire plain. So Craven, succumbing to pressure from the east and west, must have been settled by the Anglians soon afterwards. Addingham, the name means 'the farmstead of the followers of Adda', is considered to be one of the earlier Anglian settlements because of the ending - inghaem (ingahem).

Establishing the Church

The church stands on a high bluff above the river at the east end of the present village. A former rector, the Revd. W. Wrangham-Hardy, wrote, 'when the snow was on the ground, just dusting it as it so often did, you could trace the lines of the early British circle, presumably some sort of temple or place of worship within which the present church is built'. The circle is a ditch, now mostly filled in. Its eastern end was discovered by Mrs. H.E.J. le Patourel during excavations made

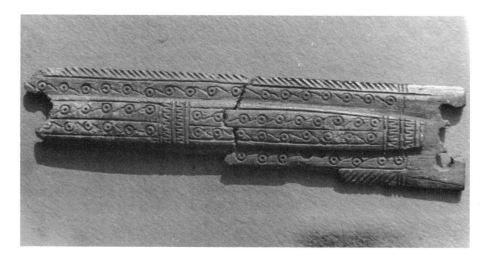

Decorated bone plaque, formerly thought to be a Viking comb case. *H. Holmes.*

in 1972-74. Unfortunately it is impossible to date it but it is possible that the church is built inside a pre-existing Iron Age ditch. In the churchyard one or two north-south burials have been found, without grave goods, so were presumably very early Christian burials.

In the middle layers of the infilled ditch was found an ornamental bone plaque. It was then identified as probably part of a Viking age bone comb case but Mr. Arthur MacGregor has recently examined the find and has concluded that it was probably a decorative plate, perhaps attached to the lid of a wooden box. He reports that boxes mounted with such strips occur in a variety of secular and ecclesiastical contexts from Roman times until the twelfth century and suggests that this piece dates between the late eighth and eleventh centuries. Mr. MacGregor's full report will appear in the publication of excavations at Addingham by the West Yorkshire Archaeology Service. I am most grateful to Mr. MacGregor and the Archaeology Service for permission to include this information in advance of its full publication.

In 1990 an excavation was carried out to the west of the church hall. It revealed an eighth century graveyard, at least a hundred years earlier than Wulfhere's visit to Addingham (below). The small area which was investigated contained about fifty graves. There were found the remains, or partial remains, of about eighty people. A geophysical survey of the adjoining area suggests there may be more graves not yet disturbed and there is the possibility of more graves being concealed under the church hall. The exciting discovery of this early graveyard helps to confirm the belief that Addingham could have been an early centre of Christianity. The graves, although placed in the customary east-west position, are not quite parallel but seem to have been aligned on to one point, possibly a cross, and perhaps predating any church building. The people buried are of all ages and both sexes; only one or two had signs of violence. They may, however, have been buried over a short space of time as the grave cuts are clean and would be well marked in the ground when the cemetery was in use. Radiocarbon dating of the bones suggests an eighth century date. Overlying this graveyard were mediaeval remains (see Chapter II). It is obvious that the field still holds secrets which could be revealed in the future. In the meantime every effort should be made not to harm or destroy any remains there may be underneath the grass.

The first record of Addingham appears in a letter written about the history of the Anglo-Saxon period. This was dealing with the period of the Danish invasion of 867AD.

'Inter has strages remotius se agebat episcopus Wlferius apud Addingeham in occidentali parte Eboraci in valle quae vocatur Hwerverdale super ripam fluminis Hwerf inter Oteleiam et castellum de Scipetun'

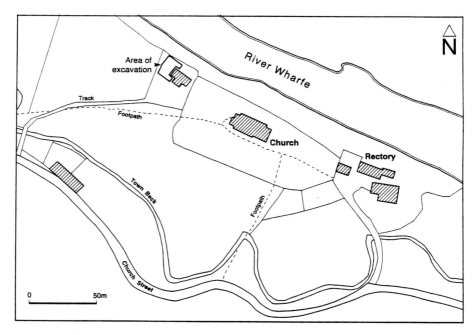

The Church and excavations of the early Anglo-Saxon cemetery. *WYAS.*

(While these bloody struggles were going on Bishop Wulfhere kept aloof residing at Addingham in the western part of Yorkshire in the valley which is called Wharfedale on the banks of the river Wharfe between Otley and the castle of Skipton).

So wrote Symeon of Durham about 1130 in a letter on the history of the Church in the North of England. The Archbishop fled from York to avoid the fighting and confusion of the warring factions of both Angles and Danes. The Archbishop owned an extensive property in Wharfedale centred on Otley of which Addingham was the most westerly portion. That he was able to live in Addingham implies that there was both a church and a hall. It is the speculation about the location of these possible foundations which make the surroundings of the church so important.

As we have seen by 867AD Addingham belonged to the Archbishop of York's estates. Can we go back even further? The recently discovered cemetery or graveyard carries the Christian presence back a further hundred years but there are possibilities of an even earlier origin.

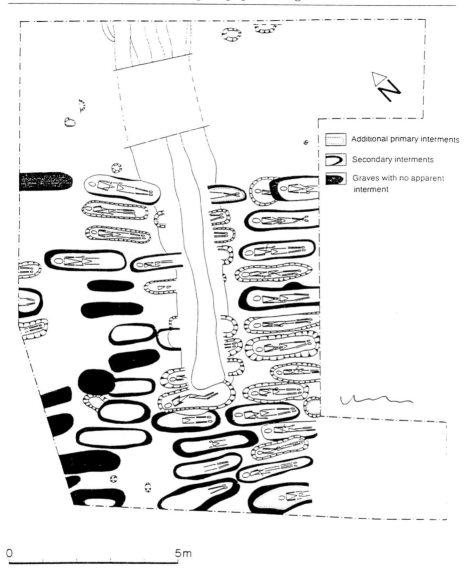

Additional primary interments

Secondary interments

Graves with no apparent
interment

0   5m

The position of the Anglo-Saxon graves. *WYAS,* previously published *YAS* (1992).

Ecgfrith of Northumbria in 678AD presented land to St. Wilfrid at Ripon. It is known that these lands belonging to Ripon were later transferred to York so it is possible, even probable, that the Otley estates of York (including Addingham) were part of the lands originally given to Wilfrid. In which case we can carry the origins of the village and its church back at least to 678AD which is within about sixty years of the defeat of the British territories of Elmet and Craven.

As to the later pre-conquest history of the church a stone cross shaft was discovered in late 1947 during the digging of a trench to the south of the church towards the Town Beck. This stone is now inside the church. It was a freestanding shaft which once had a wheelhead and it is still possible to see where this has been broken off. There are much worn vine scrolls on the back and faint carvings on the sides. The base is chamfered to fit into a socket. The symbolism of the main picture has been interpreted as a doomsday scene. The cross has resemblances to others found in the north-west in Cheshire and Cumbria and is attributed to the Viking period. A crossbase of rather rough and crude design, and of similar date, still remains in the churchyard. It was noted and drawn in Nathaniel and Henry Johnstone's notebooks on their visit in 1669.

0   20   40   cm

The Viking cross shaft. From *Viking Age Sculpture* (© R. N. Bailey) redrawn by Mark Whyman.

Addingham continued as part of the archbishop's estates until the reign of Ethelred. Oswald, incumbent of the see of York from 972AD to 992AD, lamented 'these are the villages which have been taken from Otley: the first is Addingham (Hattincham), the second Ilkley, the third Menston...' (in all thirteen places). 'I had them all until Ethelred ascended then St. Peter was robbed of them.' Although Oswald later recovered most of his lost lands he never recovered Addingham. By the time of the Norman Conquest most of Addingham was in the hands of Earl Edwin, the powerful Earl of Mercia and brother-in-law of King Harold who was killed in 1066 at the battle of Hastings.

References

Hinde, J., (ed), 1867. '*Symeonis Dunelmensis opera et collectanea*'. Surtees Society, Vol 51 (London)

Bannister, J., 1985. 'Vegetational and Archaeological History of Rombald's Moor, West Yorkshire'. Leeds University Ph.D. thesis (unpublished)

Cowling, E.T., 1946. '*Rombalds Way*, a Prehistory of Mid Wharfedale' (Otley)

Hartley, B., 1988. '*Roman Ilkey*' (Ilkley)

Ilkley Archaeology Group, 1986. '*The Carved Rocks on Rombalds Moor*' (Wakefield)

Faull, M.L., and Moorhouse, S., (eds), 1981. '*West Yorkshire: An Archaeological Survey to AD 1500*' (Wakefield)

Bailey, R.N., 1980. '*Viking Age Sculpture in Northern England*'. (London)

Whitaker, T.D., 1878. 'The History and Antiquities of the Deanery of Craven, in the County of York'. 1878. (London)

YAS., 1992. 'Mediaeval Yorkshire'. *YAJ* Vol. 21, pp. 22-25. (Leeds)

Robertson, A.J., 1956. 'Anglo-Saxon Charters', 2nd Edition, p.110, No 54 (Cambridge)

Whyman, M., 1985. 'Early Ecclesiastical Topography of Mid-Wharfedale' York University Ph.D. thesis (unpublished)

Smith, A.H., 1961. '*The Place Names of the West Riding of Yorkshire*'. Pt VI, p. 57. (Cambridge)

Smyth, A.P., 1959. '*Scandinavian York and Dublin*'. *Vol 1*. (Dublin)

Whitlock, D., (ed), 1959. '*English Historical Documents I*'. (London)

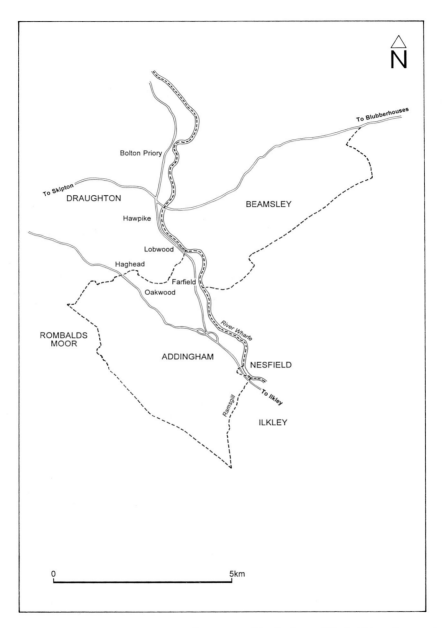

Addingham showing its relationship to adjacent townships in the twelfth & thirteenth centuries. The boundary between Addingham & Draughton is the one described in a charter granted by Alice de Romille about 1155 AD.

Chapter 2

Mediaeval Addingham 1066-1611

THE evidence for the Mediaeval and Tudor periods from the Domesday Book to the accession of James I of England to the throne in 1603 is fragmentary and dispersed through time and placed in many documents. I have used many different types of archives to try to make a story. The Domesday Book, despite all its difficulties, is the foundation and beginning. The narrative continues using a few ancient charters and deeds which are sufficient evidence, with later field names, to reconstruct the topography of the land. Various lists — tax lists and military lists — help to see the lives of the people whose wills remain in York (in the Borthwick Institute for Historical Research). The wills reveal how men and women thought of their religion, their heirs and the correct disposal of their property, together with many details of their possessions.

The Domesday Book

Everyone knows of the changes brought about by the Norman Conquest and these are clearly shown in the book drawn up for William the Conqueror. The Domesday Book was compiled in 1086 to inform William of those who had rights over all the land of the realm and how much tax it might yield. The entries for Addingham are difficult to interpret. Of the six entries two are straightforward and state that in Odingeham the King (William) held two carucates of land (a measure of taxable land, supposed to be the amount of land a full plough team of eight oxen could plough in a year. Theoretically this was 120 acres but it varied widely from one place to another. It may have been nearer to 80 acres in this district. (A bovate or oxgang, which we shall meet later, was one eighth of a carucate.) This land was part of the large Manor of Bolton-in-Craven which had belonged to Earl Edwin. It was all waste (i.e. untilled). This was in Craven.

Two more entries describe land held in 1086 by Gislebert Tison at Edidha or Ediham. In the time of King Edward (1066) it had been held by a Saxon called Gamelbarn and came under the heading of the West Riding. There seems to be some confusion about the amount of land. It is written variously as two carucates and one carucate and there is land for one plough (or half a plough) worth ten shillings (or five shillings). Here was also wood pasture one league long and half a league wide. We cannot explain the inconsistencies; perhaps the clerk was muddled or confused.

It is clear that the main part of Addingham was 'waste', that is that it had once been cultivated but was now untilled and, by implication, uninhabited. But somewhere, in one corner, a plough was being worked. The wood pasture was quite extensive and may have been near Highfield whose fields were called Oakwood or Outwood until the eighteenth century. Many other fields are called by names which indicate clearing of woods to make fields (Ridding, Stubbing etc.).

Shortly after the Domesday survey the King granted his land in Bolton, including Addingham and Draughton to the de Romilles at Skipton and Gislebert Tison's lands were added to the Percy Fee. Both the de Romilles and the Percys granted their shares of Addingham to the Vavasour family and thus the two parts of the township were united under one Lord of the Manor. The Vavasours held Addingham as owners and Lords of the Manor and did not relinquish all their interest until 1715.

Shaping the Boundaries

The survival of the village depended not only on arable land for growing corn crops and meadow and pasture for maintaining animals but also on woodland for fuel, timber for houses and barns. The moors and wastes provided peat, rushes, heather and stone. All the land had its place in supplying the needs of families. How completely the boundaries of each township were determined before the Norman Conquest is difficult to tell.

The northern boundary, the swift flowing River Wharfe, was a natural barrier only breached in one place where one field was, until recently, in Nesfield presumably as the result of some alteration in the course of the river. The eastern boundary was probably then, as it is now, determined by the course of a small beck known as Ramsgill, a tributary of the Wharfe. The southern boundary along the top of Rombalds Moor was probably not defined. It was not fully marked out until the enclosure of Addingham Moor in 1873. Skipton Castle claimed some jurisdiction over the Moor and made a small charge for what they called 'escape of beasts'. The western boundary was the best documented in the early days. This boundary between Draughton and Addingham was also a boundary of the Manor of Bolton — the part which Alice de Romille of Skipton granted to Bolton Priory about 1155. The boundary is described in some detail and is

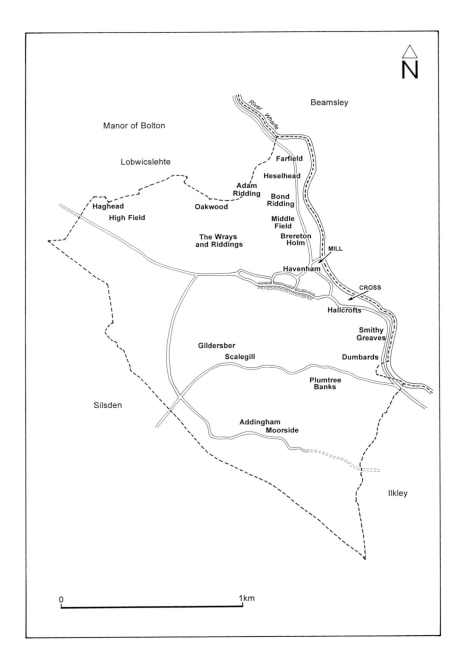

Places and fields named in the early charters and deeds. *Drawn by WYAS.*

basically the line as it still is today. The grant, translated from the Latin, says '...all the Manor of Bolton...following these bounds, namely from *Lumgil* below the hedge *(haia)* which is called *Lobwith* as it goes to the marsh *(mora)* which is called *Lobwithslec*, by the same *Lumgile* as far as the waters of the Wharfe...'. It then recounts the boundary upstream until it returns to *Lumgilheved* in the marsh next to *Lobwith*. This boundary can be identified today from Haghead to the Wharfe at the west of Farfield Hall.

The now small beck which flows down the west side of Farfield must be the *Lumgile* of this charter. *Lobwith* is Lobwood (or Lobard as it is pronounced locally). The *haia* must be Haghead. A much later boundary account mentions an ancient ditch or fence referring to this part of the boundary. The ditch has almost disappeared to be replaced by a handsome wall which still follows the ancient boundary line.

All tithes of corn, hay and increase of stock grown within this boundary, as also from some land in Beamsley (in Addingham parish), were paid to the Addingham church.

The Lords of the Manor

The chief seat of the Vavasours was Hazlewood near Tadcaster. They held the whole of Addingham and, as the custom was, they probably built or rebuilt the church, built a cornmill with its weir across the river and erected a hall or manor house. Some of the early members of the family must have lived in the hall as various deeds were drawn up and signed at Addingham.

The hall was built on the bank near the church as we are told by Nathaniel Johnstone who visited Addingham in 1669. 'The manor house stood near the church on Wharfe brow and, the land being worn away by the river, the hall fell so that there is nothing now remaining of it'. The exact site of the hall has of course completely disappeared. The names Hallcroft and Hall Orchard (or Lord's Orchard) indicate land surrounding the hall.

A drawing on a map of Nesfield, 1585, (at Chatsworth) shows the manorial complex with the rectory and church. Perhaps the hall peeps out behind and a circular tower may be part of the hall. It is unlikely that the tower is part of the church since, as far as we know, the church had no tower before 1758 when a new one was added.

When William Vavasour died in 1313 an Inquisition Post Mortem was held, (an enquiry into the possesssions he owned at the time of his death). It states that in Addingham he had a capital messuage (a chief residence) with sixty acres of land in demesne (for his own use) and twelve acres of meadow. There were two

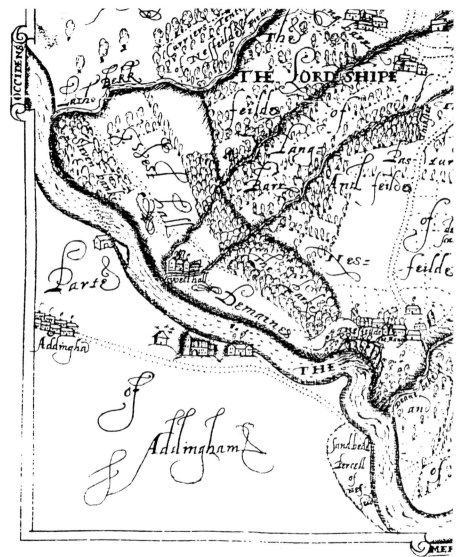

A map of Nesfield and part of Addingham made in 1585. The part of Addingham shown includes the Church, rectory or hall, and mediaeval dovecote. The corn mill is shown up river and in the corner the beginning of the village houses.

and a half carucates of land in bondage, a wood, a watermill, a fulling mill and the advowson of the church. All these were held from Robert de Clifford of Skipton who was his overlord. There were also four bovates of land held from Henry de Percy all held by knight service.

This most interesting survey tells us certain facts about the village, the hall, the church and the mills (both the corn mill and the fulling mill were probably driven by the same waterwheel) and were all built on land of the Honour of Skipton (earlier part of the de Romilles' land) which was part of Earl Edwin's land before the Conquest. The sixty acres in demesne and the meadowland were farmed by the Vavasours to provide for their own household. The two and a half carucates in bondage were worked by tenants known as bondmen or villeins who could not leave their farms without permission but could be sold to others together with their families and chattels. William Vavasour thought sufficiently of Robert, his forester in Addingham, to bequeath him twenty shillings in his will, also leaving Thomas of Addingham one mark (thirteen shillings and fourpence).

About 1205 Sir Robert Vavasour had obtained from King John permission to make a park and to hunt game which his grandson William also kept. This was the park in which Canon William of Appleton from Bolton Abbey was caught poaching deer! The park has long been dispersed among the other farms in Addingham. It was to the south of the 'Street' in the glacial meltwater valley between the Southfield and Gildersber lands. We cannot find its early boundaries but what a suitable rough valley for deer and other wild animals. This long strip of land was sold in six parts by the Vavasours in 1619. It was then known as the 'Street' or 'Bullcommon' although one field is still called 'The Park'.

Sometimes the rents from Addingham went towards the dower of widows of the Percy, Clifford or Vavasour families. At other times the manor was rented out. John de Rythre ('King's Yeoman') and his wife Alianora held the manor in 1305 when he was granted free warren (the right to hunt) in the park. The conditions of his lease stated that he was allowed to treat the land as he wished and to improve it; that action could not be taken against him for waste except in the case of houses, large oaks or the expulsion of villeins (turning the tenants out).

As time passed the Vavasours seem to have spent little time in Addingham. They divided the demesne land and dispersed it among their tenants regarding the land as a source of revenue rather than a provider of food. They may have held on to the cornmill and also kept the advowson of the church in their own control although there were times when it was leased out. Leonard Vavasour was appointed rector about 1483; by this time the church was probably in poor repair and it is assumed that it was he who restored the nave roof and also added the north aisle. William Knolles in 1547 desired his body to be buried within the new quire (?choir) at the head of the new ylinge (aisling) within the Church of St. Peter.

The People of the Manor

What of the ordinary people who lived in the village? They are not so easy to see as their lords. Their lives were humdrum lived out against seed time and harvest, felling a tree, ploughing a small assart, enduring dearth and famine or rejoicing in a good harvest. In the course of time they would alter the whole landscape.

Although their work is not well recorded unless the rolls of the mediaeval 'court leets' survive (which they do not for Addingham) there are other useful records. Tax lists can be found, some more complete than others. There are army lists, deeds and charters. Perhaps the most informative of all are the last wills and testaments left by both men and women. The wills were proved in the Archbishop's court at York where they were copied into large books which still survive and can be consulted.

We do not know for certain where many of the people lived. Thirteenth century pottery was found in a mediaeval farmyard on Church Street as well as on the moorside. There are indications of settlements, long lost, out in the fields. A field name 'Woodhouse Walls', on the moorside, may have been the site of a mediaeval house. Nearby, in Plumtree Banks, are the building platforms of a complex iron smelting site with at least two other houses.

Few early records survive but a small group of deeds and charters have been published. They date between 1200 and 1400AD. A number of parties to the transactions and some of the witnesses were Addingham men. One of the witnesses to an early deed was Thomas, Parson of Addingham, the earliest named rector. Henry the Hunter and Jordan the Hunter were involved in grants of land, as was Peter son of Paul the carpenter. Was he Peter Cook, the father of Adam, who was named in a deed of a similar date? Was Adam the Adam Sorheles whose name appears in a number of deeds? Robert Potter of Addingham bought land from the daughters of Adam Brereton (or Breirton). Perhaps Robert Potter's son was the Thomas Potter of Addingham who complained bitterly that he was set upon in Otley by Richard de Bayldon, John son of Adam de Otley and John son of Robert, the clerk of Otley, and was assaulted, beaten, wounded, ill-treated and robbed of goods and chattels worth a hundred shillings.

We hear of Agnes, wife of Ralph the smith, and Simon the smith *(fabro)* of Gildehus. These were probably not blacksmiths but were smelting and working iron. Many heaps of cinders, the dross and remains of early iron working were still evident when Nathaniel Johnstone visited Addingham in 1669.

In the late fourteenth century a poll tax was imposed on all people over sixteen years of age. The imposition of this tax was one of the causes of Wat Tyler's rebellion of 1381. In Yorkshire the most complete surviving list is that of 1379. This list shows that twenty-nine men, with their wives, paid tax. They all paid fourpence, the standard rate for the villein (peasant). The exception was William Manne, fuller, who paid the craftsman's rate of sixpence. Presumably the fulling mill mentioned at the beginning of the century was still working.

At this time surnames were just being assumed and becoming hereditary but many were still known as 'son of' or by the place from which they came. Ten men came from other places as far away as Lede (Lead, east of Leeds), Warley and Crosby (in Lancashire). Another eleven were called 'son of'. Some had descriptive names such as Robertus Webstre (a weaver). There was also a woodman. Thomas de Gyldesbergh and Thomas del Grene are surnames found also in older deeds. One name which occurs for the first time is Hardwick, sometimes written as Herdwick, a family which remained for many years.

National tax lists are also available. There is a volume on the Craven tax lists between 1510 and 1547. A list for 1522 gives twenty one names for Addingham (there should be more but the first page is missing). Most were assessed on small sums from 3s to 26s4d. William Waide th'elder paid 40s on an assessment of £20. Twenty-three people paid the lay subsidy of 1543; many were names familiar in Addingham. John Hardwick, with the highest assessment, paid 12s., on the other hand George Turner, John Robinson and William Lyster paid only 2d each. Christopher Wayde (12d) and Margaret Waide, widow, (3s) will be heard of again as members of an important family. John Hardwick of Addingham was appointed head collector for Staincliffe for October 1545 and also collected the third assessment due in February 1546.

A different type of list is the military muster roll. There is a list of men said to have been mustered by the Cliffords to fight at Flodden Field in 1513. Nine men went from Addingham 'horsed and harnessed at the town's cost'. William Wade, their leader, was 'able, horsed and harnishd' and six of the men were archers. A later and much larger muster was made at Bracewell in 1539 where all able men from Craven aged seventeen and over met. Thirty-five men went from Addingham. Ten of them rode horseback and seven of these were 'furnished' with the complete light armour worn by this equivalent of the Home Guard. The body armour consisted of a *Jak* which was a leather jacket with metal plates sewn on; a *Salit* or light helmet protected the head; a *Gorget* protected the neck and a *Splence* was worn over the elbows and arms. These pieces of armour were often left as heirlooms or handed on by will. John Green in 1556 left his *sword* and *buckler* to one son and his *jacke* and *sallett* to his other son. Probably the thirty-five men who went to Bracewell were the whole able and fit adult male population of the village which speaks of very slow growth from the twenty-nine couples who paid the poll tax 150 years earlier.

Wills can be most revealing documents. Although many are very simple or merely emphasise the inheritance customs of the Manor others show religious beliefs, some earlier beliefs continuing after the Reformation. There was generosity to the poor in the custom of leaving alms to be given to the poor either at the funeral or out of the estate of the deceased. The range and variety of goods and chattels which the testator might have at his or her disposal is often quite surprising.

About seventy wills survive made by the inhabitants of Addingham between 1329 and 1612. The preamble to them shows how people conformed to the religion of the time. A few still used the unreformed phrases of the earlier church but many took the Reformation in their stride. In earlier days money was often left to the church to pay for masses for the souls of the testators and their ancestors. Sometimes the best animal was left to the church. Money was also left to the shrine of St. Robert of Knaresborough who was a popular and well-known local saint.

It is clear from the wills that most holdings were leaseholds for terms of years. A man often directed that his goods be divided into three parts, one part for his wife, one for the children and the third to pay his debts. Bequests of livestock and also clothing were often made. Cows called 'Huswif', 'Cherry' and 'Wilde' were named; grandchildren were often given a gimmer (female) lamb. Agnes Holmes, widow, (1587) left to her youngest son 'one brown branded cow and six sheep to make his cheyse' (cheese). Grace Lofthouse (1583) amongst other possessions bequeathed 'a great arke (a wooden chest for storing oatmeal), her best petticoat and gown, naperye (household linen) and an old petticoat, '...the expenses of my buryall to be very liberall with honestre'. Agnes Heardweeke of Addingham Moor Raw (1608) made a detailed list of bequests including 'certayne lynnen cloths, a boulster, one featherbed, one coverlett, two blankets and four separate parcels of linen'.

A few wills mention tools used for making textiles. William Atkinson of Alme Green (1600) left 'a lowme (loom) of three years old, a pair of walker shears (for trimming the nap of cloth) and woolcombs'. James Gryne (Green) (1590) had a pair of narrow looms and a pair of healds. Richard Lister (1584) specified that his son be brought up at school in learning and not to be used and handled 'lyke an hyreling' at home.

Some of the makers of wills had obviously travelled and had connections and interests in other places. Henry Hardwyke (1426) left 6s8d to the fabric of St. Peter's, York. John Waud (1439) left 12d to the house of St. Robert of

Knaresborough. William Holgate (1584) and Christopher Silson (1586) owed money to people from Fowbrigge (Ferrybridge?), Hippom (Hipperholme?), Bramhope, Gargrave and Kildwick. John Dawson (1591) bequeathed lands at Monk Fryston and Christopher Holmes of Addingham (1594) was buried at Whitkirk. All these men must have had stories to tell of their travels. Anthony Wade, of Plumtree Banks, travelled much further for he wrote from Ostend in 1596/7 where he was accompanying his cousin Thomas Maud of Hollin Hall, Ilkley. His letter was to William Saxey, a clerk of the Exchequer in London.

Henry VIII's Reformation seems to have been accepted without difficulty although we know, from other sources, that two brothers of the Kirkman family remained adherents of the old faith. They were educated at the Roman Catholic college of Douai in France before returning to England in 1578. Richard Kirkman was arrested in 1582 and on confessing that he was a Catholic priest was tried and executed at York. The Roman Catholic church founded in the village in 1927 is dedicated to 'Our Lady and the English Martyrs'. Richard Kirkman was one of those who suffered martyrdom for his faith.

The Fields and Farms of the Township

Southfield, Farfield and Highfield are reminders of the arable fields cultivated in common over many centuries. There may have been a Northfield and a Middle-field also. Later deeds show that some of the land to the east of the township — the Holmes, the Hallcrofts and the Dumbards in particular — were also farmed in strips as common arable field, but, where we should expect that these should be called the Eastfield this does not seem to have been so. These fields to the east of the village, which is the most fertile land, may have been the old demesne land divided into strips and shared among the farms of the township. As we approach the east end of the Main Street the 'rig and furrow', indicative of mediaeval ploughing, is particularly easy to see at Town End (formerly Town Gate), Thack Wood Ing (now the cricket field) and the Dumbards further east.

Most of the evidence for the common, or open, fields comes from seventeenth century documents and we must be wary of using them as indications of earlier conditions. The number of arable fields can be explained in different ways, perhaps the most likely being that all were not in use at the same time. For instance only one deed mentions the Southfield which may have been enclosed before 1600. Certainly the Ley Closes were in grass by that time. On the other hand there are indications that the Oakwood was being taken into the Highfield as late as the eighteenth century.

The only evidence of the open arable fields in mediaeval times is in a deed

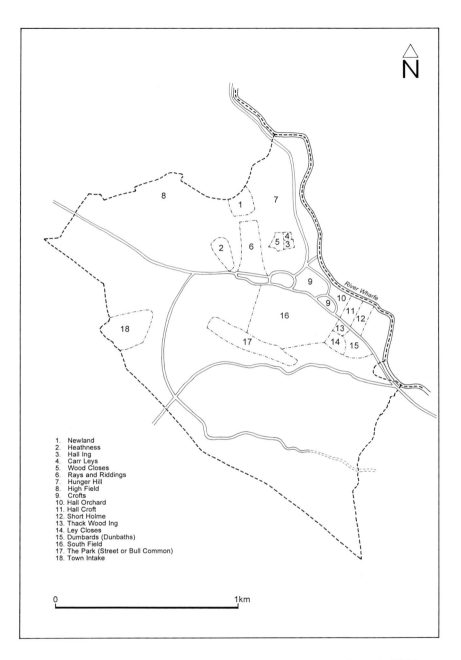

1. Newland
2. Heathness
3. Hall Ing
4. Carr Leys
5. Wood Closes
6. Rays and Riddings
7. Hunger Hill
8. High Field
9. Crofts
10. Hall Orchard
11. Hall Croft
12. Short Holme
13. Thack Wood Ing
14. Ley Closes
15. Dumbards (Dunbaths)
16. South Field
17. The Park (Street or Bull Common)
18. Town Intake

0   1km

The approximate position of the mediaeval fields in Addingham. *Drawn by WYAS.*

dealing with only five acres of land but these are in sixteen different locations and name nineteen separate pieces of land. The deed is between Adam de Brereton and Sir John Vavasour. It is undated but is witnessed by Jordan the Hunter and Adam Sorheles, probably about 1230. The land is listed as 'Half an acre which lies above Lobwicslehte and extends towards Lobwic, one rood (there are four roods in an acre) in the same field which lies within Smaledales and extends over Heselwodgile, one rood in the same field which lies within Overwralandes, one rood in Netherwra, one and a half roods above Mikeldales, half a rood above Aftwaldes, one rood in the field of Norfeld which lies in Byerbladethyart, one and a half roods which lie in Geoffrey's assart, one rood in the same field which extends above that assart, one rood which lies above Heselheved, one rood which lies above Grettilandes, half an acre in culture which is called Brereton Holme between the grantor's land and the water, one rood in a culture called Havenham, half an acre in Suhfeld on the east side which extends towards Scalegile, half an acre in the same field which extends to Henry's Cross, half a rood in a culture which is called Ricardcroft which extends towards the land of Richard Queinte'.

The land seems to be named in order from the west end at Farfield to the east at Henry's Cross (Crossend) and an unidentified Ricardcroft. Some of the field names are now lost but a number are still recognisable. The Rays (Overwralandes and Netherwra), Britton Holme (Brereton Holme), Aynholme (Havenham) and Cross End (Henry's Cross) are still names in use.

Other deeds name clearings called assarts or riddings. These are mainly near the boundary with Draughton. Their location is described in detail; one from the ditch of Lobwic to the assart which William Dispensator once held; Adam Sorheles was given an assart below Lobwid which his father, Peter Cook, holds for life; another assart was in Lobwithgate which once had belonged to Peter le Bond. There are still fields at Farfield called Adam Ridding and Bond Ridding. Langeryding, Wraryding and Northryding are named in a deed of about 1300. We can tell where these lay because one of the old lanes into the fields was called Long Ridding Lane (now known as Lang Leading Lane). There are other Ridding names at the east side of the village and there are other woodland names such as School Wood, Broad Ash, Stubbing and Springs (this means young tree growth springing up and has nothing to do with water). All these names indicate a former heavy cover of woodland.

One more piece of land is named in the early charters and deeds and this is fifteen acres of land at Gildersber lying between Hutredville and Scaleville (Hutredgill and Scalegill). Simon the Smith lived there. This land was granted to Henry the Hunter and, after his death, to Jordan the Hunter. Scalegill can be identified from nineteenth century maps. Hart Rydding is the modern name of

Chapter 3

The Seventeenth Century

The Land Surveys of 1611 and 1612

IN 1611 Richard Newby made a survey of the Addingham land. It was very unusual as it seems to have been commissioned by the tenants and was entitled 'a particular survey of all the landes and groundes of William Vavasour esq., inclosed from the moors and commons within his Manor of Addingham'. This survey was made to establish who held land in the old demesne lands of the manor and who had cattlegates in the old stinted pastures. (Cattlegates were the number of cattle a tenant was allowed to graze in one of these pastures. The pastures were 'stinted' because there were only a limited number of cattle allowed to graze in each. The length of time for which they were allowed to graze might also be limited.) What was the acreage (in statute acres) of each tenement and the equivalent acreage of the cattlegates?

The former demesne lands, those lands once farmed by the Vavasours for themselves for their own profit but now let out amongst their tenants, were named as the Hallinges, the Hall Orchards, Hallcrofts, Dunbers, Shortholme, Sandylands, Half Acres, Crooked Lands, Thackwood Ing and 'no more unless the Park be'.

Eighteen of the tenants had neither parts of the demesne land nor cattlegates. The total acreage of their farms was 507 acres; many of them seem to have been tenants living on the Moorside. A further thirty-seven tenants had both demesne land and cattlegates, their acreage coming to 949 acres. There were four stinted pastures; the Town Intack of 105 acres with 61 cattlegates; Mr. Vavasour's part of Ley close, 25 acres with 23 cattlegates; Haythnes (Heathness) New Intack , 60 acres with $42\frac{1}{2}$ plus $\frac{2}{3}$ cattlegates; finally Newland, 40 acres with $22\frac{1}{2}$ cattlegates. At the end of the survey it stated that neither the highways, the Sandbed, the Bullcommon or any fence were measured.

The following year a further survey was made, this time for Mr. Vavasour, valuing the land of all the tenants. The land was not listed, as was usually the case, under their strips, closes or holdings in the fields but was valued by the quality of the soil. This must have been one of the first soil surveys ever made.

The land was divided into three types, 'a threefold proportional particular expressing severall quantities of their said tenements according to a threefold nature or quallitie of the grounde belonging the same (that is to say) the first particular mentioning the quantity of the worst grounde as of Haythness, Highfield, Newland, Town Intake and suchlike. The second of the middle or indifferent grounde as Suffields, Wrays, Riddings, Woodcloses, Hallings, Carrs, Hungerhills and suchlike, and the third of the best grounde as the Crofts, Bargh (Bark), Hallfields and such other Low Grounde'. The worst ground was valued at 1s8d the acre, the middle at 3s4d and the best at 5s the acre yearly value. The ground of each of the thirty-six tenements was measured and valued in detail. This value was probably not the rent actually to be paid; in many cases the mediaeval rents had never been raised and the landlords got their money by other devices such as entry fines (money paid at the making of a lease).

The farms on the Moorside were also valued (with the exception of those belonging to Ermysted's School and to the Wade family). There were nineteen tenements whose best land was valued at 4s per acre, the middle land at 2s9d an acre and the worst land at 1s6d an acre. It is possible that a map accompanied this survey because there are symbols at the side of each tenant's name.

As the survey made clear the best land of all lies roughly from the present Bark Lane eastward towards the river and took in nearly all the demesne land. The best land on the Moorside was worth little more than the second best of the lower land and these differences still show up today. The intrinsic quality of the land is unaltered and the modern soil survey still shows the same pattern.

The Wades held fourteen acres of the old demesne land as part of their freehold and the parson had five acres of the same as his glebe. The Wades also paid a free rent for Plumtree Banks and Reynard Ing. A few small Intakes were also considered freehold lands.

Adjoining the Wade's farm was the block of land belonging to Ermysted's Grammar School. This land is first mentioned when Peter Toller endowed the Chantry Chapel of St. Nicholas in Skipton Church in 1492. It was later given by Ermysted to endow the Grammar School in Skipton in 1548 (see p. 23). The one and a half tenements given by Peter Toller had grown to five when the Grammar School was founded. The extra land most probably came from the intaking of common land from the moor. Evidence in a lawsuit of 1700 says 'a considerable part of the lands consisted of Intakes and new enclosures taken from a large common called Rumilly (Rombalds) More'. The farms grew to be seven in number at the time of the lawsuit but finally some consolidation took place and the land was divided between four farms – Cragg House, Overgate Croft, School Wood and Low Brockabank.

The Vavasour land sales

The 1612 survey was the preliminary of great change for in 1618 William and Thomas Vavasour decided to sell their lands in Addingham. They ran into difficulties with the original sale because the land was entailed (had to be inherited by the male heir) so it was transferred back to them and reconveyed to trustees who then completed the transactions.

The first sale in 1619 involved 45 messuages (farms) and two cottages and lands in Addingham. This was followed in 1620/21 by the sale of 20 messuages, 8 cottages, one watermill, 20 barns, 20 gardens, 160 acres of land (arable), 60 acres of meadow, 280 acres of pasture, 200 acres of heath and ling and 800 acres of moor. Reserved at these sales were the manorial rights – that is the soil of the commons and such mineral rights as of coal, iron, stone and limestone; also hawking, hunting and the right to hold courts.

Specifically excepted from the sale were the Street or Bullcommon and parcels of waste called the Mill Sandbeds, the Smithy Greaves and 120 acres 'whereof 23 acres are already limitted and sett out in divers and several places in the east side and the residue of the 120 acres are limitted and agreed taken after the west side of the commons which part and divide the Lordshipp of Silsden belonging to the Earl of Cumberland and the Lordship of Addingham'.

Agreements must have been made for the partition and sale of the Bullcommon or Street 'in thirty parts to be divided according to the nomber of auncient oxgang land in Addingham'. The four stinted pastures and part of the Hall Ing were also divided and sold. We find such sales as 'three full parts of another field called Hathenesse the same into forty two parts to be divided'. 'One part of another Great Close of Newland in twenty one parts to be divided'. 'Three whole parts of one great close of pasture called the Intake into three score and three parts to be divided'. These are very near to the number of stints already agreed and may mainly have been sold to the stint holders of the time. The land of mediaeval farms was divided into strips of a quarter or half an acre scattered through big arable fields, Farfield, Highfield, Middlefield, Southfield and possibly other fields. The lease of Adam de Brereton (p. 17) in the thirteenth century shows this well. Even at the time of the land sales in 1618 some of the farms were still in strips or 'selions' of land. Such a farm was bought from Wm Vavasour by Robert Lawnde, clothyer, on 28th December, 1618, whose lands included six different strips in Highfield, five in Middlefield, five in Farfield, one in Southfield and one dole of meadow in Thackwooding Ing. He had also closes at Bargh (Bark) Lane and Winebeck.

The sale of all the farms enabled the new owners to exchange these strips and gather them together into bigger blocks which made them more convenient to work although the process was slow. During the next half century the farmers re-organised their farms. As farmers of strips in the open fields their farmhouses had lined the Main Street, with a scatter of old farms along the Moorside and the old road to Skipton (the present day Moor Lane). A great and continuing exchange, buying and consolidating of the various strips of land took place, both of the strips in the open fields and the small portions of the stinted pastures – a process which led to the formation of 'closes'. The farms along the Moorside had probably always been in closes.

As the farms consolidated, albeit with closes scattered around the township and not always adjacent to one another, some new farmhouses were built in the new closes and thus we get farmhouses on the sites we see today at Farfield, Holme House, Street House and Southfield farms. The farms were no bigger, on average, than they had been earlier but it was no longer such a trail to take plough teams to plough the small and scattered strips, so there was a great saving in time. Also it was possible to fence these closes and farm them as each man wished; to drain, lime and improve the land. There was another rather surprising result of this re-organisation in that no more of the commons, moors and wastes were enclosed and they continued as common land coming right down to the Main Street at Townhead until the final enclosure award of 1873. The first Ordnance Survey, or Tithe map, of 1845 shows unfenced roads across the then common towards Silsden and Moor Lane.

This re-organisation of the farms does not seem to have changed the number of working farms nor is it clear whether the 120 acres reserved out of the land sales were ever enclosed or sold. The growth of the village came much later with the growth of other trades, particularly textiles, as the Main Street was infilled with cottages between the old farmhouses.

The Constable's Accounts

With the relaxation of control of the Manor, after the land sales, the yearly accounts of the officers of the township begin to survive. From 1620 onwards we have the accounts of both the Constable and the Overseers of the Poor. Although a number are missing and a few are incomplete there are sufficient to illustrate the condition and problems of the inhabitants. It was the duty of the Constable to keep order in the village and see that the law was upheld. He was unpaid and was appointed for a year, in April, when he attended the sheriff's court, usually at Skipton (occasionally at Gisburn), and received his warrant.

The accounts at the beginning of the century show payments for the repair of the cucking stool and later for the pinfold and the stocks. The pinfold was at the bottom of Stockinger Lane and the stocks were said to be near the Fleece Inn. The site of the cucking stool or ducking stool is unknown. There were monthly searches for strangers staying illegally and, occasionally, for prisoners escaped from Lancaster gaol. The Constable paid over taxes and rates at the Skipton court. The county rate was collected to maintain bridges, Walshford, Wetherby and Ilkley bridges are mentioned, also York gaol. He took also lists of Innholders, tippling houses, badgers (corn dealers) and drovers. There were many travellers along the road and a number held passes, presumably issued by Justices of the Peace. These travellers had to be helped along their journey and often their night's lodging was paid. Cripples were usually carried in carts. It may have been a case of self interest – a sort of 'pass the parcel' – if one of these travellers fell sick he might have to be maintained by the village until he was recovered and could continue his journey. Occasionally the Constable fell for a hard luck story as when Henery Dawson was given threepence on 24th December 'who was benighted and had no money'. Soldiers and even sailors travelled through. 'Samlyer (Samuel) Ward a sohlyer (soldier) who was prest (pressed) from Malham and came back by reason of sickness' was given threepence.

Another duty was to keep the town's armour in repair. This duty became more important as time went on, for in 1639 King Charles I was in the north of England preparing for an attack on Scotland. The Constable's accounts for the years 1639 and 1640 show how the local districts were affected. Each township had to provide men and arms to serve in the 'train bands' – roughly the equivalent of the Home Guard of the last war. These men were called up for training for one or two days at a time at various local places. It is clear from the accounts that they were clothed, supplied with arms and ammunition, victuals and paid their wages by the village. Their armour was mended, a sword 'scaberd' was paid for; three pikes were 'houped' (hooped); match and powder were provided for muskets, which were also mended as necessary. Clothes were also made for the men. Eight and a quarter yards of cloth were bought costing 17s7d, cap making cost 3s8d and thread and inkle (broad linen tape) used in the making 1s4d. Bandaleeros (shoulder belts for ammunition) were bought at York and they were given 'oyle bottels and cases for muskets'.

Training was carried out at various places, at Morton and Silsden where the soldiers were paid 8s for wages and 1s2d for ale. Kirsgill (an unidentified place) was also a training ground where the lieutenant was given 2s. The soldiers also travelled to Knaresborough and Ripon accompanied by the Constable who claimed 5s for his wages.

A new account was started in October possibly with a new Constable. During the winter there was less activity by the soldiers although a view of arms was held at Skipton on January 2nd, 1639/40, when six men were provided with dinners and were paid 8d each for the day. The muster master was given 1s. In the spring training was carried out for several days at Ilkley, both private and common (those who went at their own cost and the common soldiers paid by the town), this time 'upon command from Sir Nicholas Hawksworth then captayne'. That training cost £2.18.0 including powder and match, their several dinners and wages. More clothing was made; 29¼ yards of cloth; three dozen sheepskins for linings cost £3; ribbon for the captain's colours and inkle for knees and binding cost 3s6d, silk and thread 3s4d, tailor's making 16s. The accounts for the first six months came to £16.13.9 and £32.9.11 for the second half of the year, compared with the usual annual cost of £7 or £8. The ratepayers must have been hard put to find the money.

The year 1640 was no better. There were inspections at Skipton, training continued at various places including Addingham and armour had to be repaired or replaced. Six soldiers, accompanied by the Constable, travelled by Otley to Rufforth having ale at Otley, 10d, and other expenses of £3.12.0. They went on to Harewood, where they drank more ale, and on to Wetherby, where they spent the night, before proceeding to Poppleton. The Constable ate his dinner at Tadcaster (dinner 6d, Ale 2d, supper 6d, hay and oats 10d). Once again the object of the Constable making this journey seems to have been to take new clothes for he had bought two 'dozens' of blue cloth for £6 (a 'dozen' is a type of worsted), in Leeds. He must have run out of money for there is an item 'to those who lent me money in wine and sugar'.

In the autumn of 1639 the Constable had to travel to Gisburn before the Justices of the Peace, there to give an account of what 'hay, corne or other provisions might be conveniently spared for his Majestie's use during his stay in these northern parts'. There were further costs for enquiring into the possibility of buying his Majestie's venison. In 1640 there was more trouble in searching for the King's provisions; pack ponies had been sent from Halifax to Addingham and appear to have lost their way. They had to be found and sent further. There was an enquiry at Skipton about the King's carriages which may have been part of the same search. The expenses for 1640 were also very high at £31.8.9.

The next surviving accounts are for 1642 during the Civil War. Expenses were more normal again. There were a few accounts for mending and supplying armour, mending swords and buying new sword belts. John Houlmes was carried to his colours at a cost of 6d. Holmes and two brothers Musgrave, from Addingham, helped to defend the besieged Skipton Castle for the Royalists so we assume that Addingham was Royalist in its sympathies. The chief expenses in 1642 were in lodging and supporting the soldiers who were travelling along the highway, mainly to and from Skipton where the castle was besieged by Parliamentary forces.

The accounts for 1648 give an altogether more confused picture, with constant travelling of soldiers, whose lodging for the night had to be paid for. The quarters for the soldiers were usually provided by three men, most probably innkeepers. Four soldiers of Colonel Fairfax regiment spent the night at Roger Webster's and five soldiers of the 'Mager Bridse company' had one night at Thomas Brogden's costing 6s6d. John Astwick, for quartering soldiers under the command of Colonel Wet, was paid 2s8d. Thomas Brogden was also paid 10s for ale for thirty soldiers in their march to Skipton. Cornet Walmsley may have lost his life as a result of the fighting – there is a small brass in the floor of the church to his memory. He was buried there in 1652 but there is no indication on which side he served and no entry in the Parish Register.

For the rest of the century the Constable's duties settled to the old, familiar, pattern with few unusual entries. As time passed expenditure on military matters declined. Taxes and rates were collected and delivered to Skipton. Travellers with passes were paid for – in 1675 there were 104 who were given, between them, £1.9.10. 1675 saw a number of robberies, Jo Barker's house was broken into, William Stott lost a goose, Mr. Farrand lost a sheep and some hens, four sheep disappeared from Cornitt Currers, Jonothan Parkinson lost hens and geese and Anthony Mires's turkies were missing – even the ducking stool had to be searched for. This year seems to have been exceptional, no other years have similar entries. We should never have known that turkeys were kept here on farms if it had not been for the casual reference in these accounts.

Some of the Constables recorded more details about the travellers, a few of whom were on surprising journeys. In 1674 one man was on his way to Hull and another to Newcastle and, two years later, two came from Hull on their way to Penrith. Four seamen left a ship in the coast of France and four soldiers were on their way to Cockermouth. Two men came from Ireland and two soldiers came from Holland. By the end of the century the Constable's accounts were about £14 yearly – a very reasonable sum.

The Accounts of the Overseers of the Poor

The Overseers accounts start in 1620 – between then and 1700 fifty-four survive – enough to see in detail how the Poor Laws worked at parish level. In 1620 £3.8.10 was disbursed in the year, by 1699 this sum had risen to £20.19.6. Why this should have happened is not really clear. Perhaps there was some inflation, the population may have been rising though only slowly, there may have been more sick and disabled people and possibly more people were considered for relief. In 1631 five regular payments were made at 4d a week and by 1700 fifteen people were receiving regular monthly relief. The average monthly payment was 2s6d (the highest was 5s) and £2.7.0 was paid out each month.

As well as the regular allowances occasional cash payments were made often for some specific purpose such as house rent or 'house room'. Clothing was bought; Mary Boultin was given a pair of clogs worth 6d; cloth for the poor cost 10s1d and making 1s10d; Bess Spencer was given a smock. Sickness was recognised as an occasion for relief when Steven Mason was supplied with a load of coales worth 8d. The wife of Thomas Spencer was given 2s0d 'for fare of Elizabeth Thompson a poor and lame young woman for one month past'. Payment was also made in part or in full at burials of the poor.

Joshua Dawson who was overseer in 1655 was a Quaker and made particularly detailed accounts. He included at least three families who had 'catiffe' (crippled or deformed) children. Two of them were given money towards the charge of carrying them to the Wells for the recovery of their health. This must be one of the earliest records for the use of Ilkley Wells. Thomasin Bradley, widow, was given 1s0d for an 'impotent' (helpless) child. John Shires was given 2s6d for the relief of his infant after the mother was dead and later, for at least seven weeks, allowance at 1s2d a week 'by full consent of the parish'. The Shires family were particularly unfortunate. Richard Shires got 2s0d towards clothing his child's nakedness and it was he who took his crippled daughter to the Wells. Anthony Shires also had a catiffe daughter and Jane Shires was given 6d.

Joshua Dawson was overseer again in 1678, this time for the Moorside. Again his accounts are detailed. Alice Rushforth, a widow, received 12s6d for the repair of her house 'getting watling for the chimney and for watling it and glass for house window in all 2s7d'. Samuel Hartley 'in the storm' was paid 6s6d. He detailed the costs for the repair of Widow Ellen Taylor's house at Crossbank.

		s.	d.
Imp.	For taking away rubbish and old thack and laying up a ribb and eighteen spars, two men Isaac Lofthouse and my man Thomas for one day	1	6
Item	For getting spelks and leading thack from Thomas Currers one day both my men	1	9
	Two horses for leading it and for drawing it and to Constantine Lister 6d..	1	2
	For theaking and serving theaker two men three days	4	3
	For one to lead three cartloads of oat straw with one horse to Crossbank from parsonage for thacke		10
	For eight thraves of wheat straw to Thos Currer at 3d per thrave	2	0

To parson Colthurst for the like quantity as near as my man
accompts it who theaked both 2   0
For a ribb and eighteen sparrs and leading to her house as
valewed 5   0
For drawing the wheate straw which was had at parsonage
and leading it to Crossbank and horse and cart and two
horses with John Milner 1   8

                                                               19   9 (sic)

Watling	Small twigs used for reinforcing daub or plaster
Thack	Thatch
Spelk	Split wood used for binding thatch
Theak	To thatch
Theaker	Thatcher
Thrave	Normally two dozen stooks of straw

Some overseers allowed a variety of relief. Eliz Green 'at the feast' was allowed 1s0d and another at Christmas. Thos Holmes was given a peck of wheat at 1s10d, more wheat later and half a peck of oatmeal. Six cartloads of flaws (a type of peat) were led for Will Myers at a cost of 1s6d. Poor children were frequently apprenticed either to a trade or husbandry. This gave them a home with food and shelter and supposedly, at the end, an ability to earn a living. Some apprenticeship indentures survive but little appears in the accounts.

A problem which became even more serious in the next century was due to the settlement laws of 1662. A stranger in the township could be removed (to the place of his or settlement) if he, or she, did not find work within forty days. Eventually this led to whole families being sent backwards and forwards between the township of settlement (usually the place of birth) and the place of work as each was unwilling to spend money on their relief.

The year 1685 saw some change in the policy by the overseers. First they recovered a small sum of money which had been left for charitable purposes. The money was used to buy a house and land, formerly Richard Oldfield's, bought from John Crossley of Hullen Edge. This land became known as Crossley's land, or the Dole Field, and is probably the land in Moor Lane where the council houses were built. The land provided a small income and the house was let to a poor person, possibly free or at a very small rent. Another house was bought for the same purpose. Ellen Laund lived in a house consisting of a 'body stead' and one little parlour. This was occupied by Ellen Laund for her life and then seems to have been used for the poor. Anthony Ward had built a cottage in 1669 which was inherited by his daughter Sarah Green. At some unknown time this too must have been bought by the overseers and, in the early eighteenth century, was probably in use as a school. It still belongs to the township and is now known as the Old School, housing the library below and the council room above.

One house was purpose built in 1685/6 when the accounts show their intention to build. 6d was paid at the 'festing' (letting or contracting) the work of building the house at Townhead with John Wainman who was a mason. A further 2s. was paid when 'the house at Townehead was mesured and the workmen paid'. This house was built on Stamp Hill on land which belonged to the village (and still does). The ruins remain although it was lived in until this century. Originally it was a small, two-roomed, single storey house with a stone slate roof. It was, in fact, the first purpose built 'council' house in Addingham.

Charities for the Poor

Charitable people had always left money as well as goods to the poor. Money was sometimes left to be distributed at a funeral. Arthur Caterall gent., of Gatecroft, gave 5s0d to the poor of Addingham and John Tophan, in January 1635/6, bequeathed 4d each to the ten poorest housekeepers in Addingham parish. John Dawson, in January 1633/4, left the poor people of Addingham the sum of 10s0d yearly out of a piece of land called Newlands. Thomas Fieldhouse willed 20s0d to the poor of Addingham to be distributed by his wife with the help of John Hollins. A more substantial sum of £5 was left to the poor by John Dawson the younger of Farfield in June 1653. This type of legacy was easily lost and very vulnerable. The legatees and new owners often resisted the payment of a rent charge and eventually it was lost and forgotten. Anthony Ward took the precaution of entering his gifts to the poor in the Parish Register when he gave two sums, each of £5, about the year 1633, '...the use whereof to be distributed to the poorest widows...'. In this case it was intended that the principal sum should be lent at interest ('use') and the interest given to the poor. In practice the money became part of the poor rate and reduced the sum which the overseers thought it necessary to collect. One sum of £10 was lent out in 1627 on the security of two small fields, Stonebrig Close and Round Close. The principal was not paid back until 1685 and it was this that was invested in Richard Oldfield's house and land.

A further conveyance of land was made by Joshua Dawson on March 1st 1686/7. In accordance with his late father's wish he gave a small field called the Milne Close next to Addingham (corn) mill with the river Wharfe on the north and the Tenterlands on the south side. The rent of this field was again for the use of the poor. The field still belongs to the village and has given many generations of children great delight in playing in the river and fishing from the river bank.

1685/6 saw the distribution of the Earl of Thanet's great charity. The Earl was lord of Skipton Castle although he never lived there. He was childless, inherited his estates in middle age and was of a charitable disposition. The widest distribution of money in Craven took place in 1685. The numbers in each family receiving money are listed. There are thirty-four names occurring in Addingham and twenty-three on the Moorside. Of these thirty-one were living alone but large families also benefited. Thomas Mason, head of a family of eight, lived on the Moorside. He was given 2s6d as also Samuel Hartley with the like number. John Vaile in the village was also head of eight and Richard Shires of seven. There were five in the families of William Smith (2s6d) and Jane Hodgson (1s6d). These people did not pay poor rates so some 57 families (averaging 2·4 people) or 145 persons in all do not appear in the rates list. The rate list for 1696 (the nearest surviving list) has 86 names. If we assume an average of 4·75 members for the family of each ratepayer this makes a total of about 550 inhabitants in the village.

It is difficult to find details of the lives of the poor excepting for the glimpses provided by the accounts of the Overseers of the Poor. One family which is fairly well documented is that of Thomas Mason. He was the son of Stephen Mason and was baptized in Addingham on June 30th 1650. He seems to have been married before 1674 (the registers are missing for the previous four years) and had six children by 1685 when he was given 2s6d from the Earl of Thanet's charity. In that year he petitioned the Justices of the Peace for a weekly allowance and they ordered that he should have 1s0d a week. In his petition he describes himself as 'a very painful laborious man, but having five very small children am not able to reliefe them without sume assistance from the towne of Addingham'. In 1690 he made another plea that he had not been paid and the overseers were again ordered to pay him.

Thomas was a labourer. In his youth he helped his father to ditch and lay out fences for the highway as he testified in evidence in a case brought against Addingham in 1689. In 1689 he appears as a licensed alehouse keeper although which house he kept we do not know. In 1692 he was paying rent of 19s6d yearly to Roger Coates and Miss Coates for land. He died in 1697. We lose sight of most of his children although one of his sons, another Thomas, was apprenticed in husbandry in 1685. Ann, one of his daughters, died aged 21 and Stephen, one of his sons, died in 1724 – both were unmarried. What happened to his widow and the rest of the family is not known.

Roads and Tracks

The countryside in former times, as still today, was criss-crossed with roads and tracks. Roads as we know them were non-existent. In most cases they were

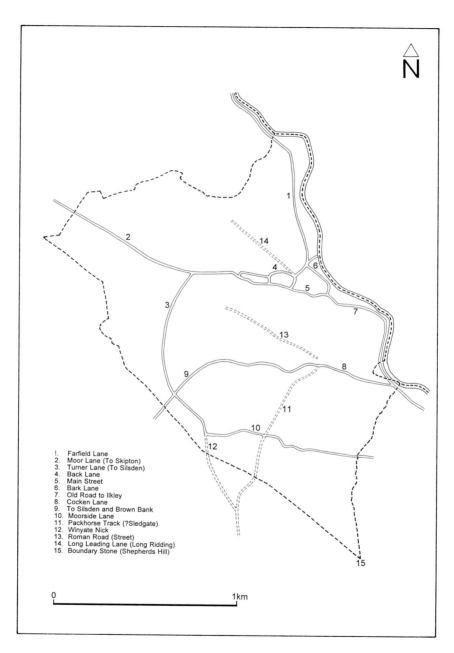

1. Farfield Lane
2. Moor Lane (To Skipton)
3. Turner Lane (To Silsden)
4. Back Lane
5. Main Street
6. Bark Lane
7. Old Road to Ilkley
8. Cocken Lane
9. To Silsden and Brown Bank
10. Moorside Lane
11. Packhorse Track (?Sledgate)
12. Winyate Nick
13. Roman Road (Street)
14. Long Leading Lane (Long Ridding)
15. Boundary Stone (Shepherds Hill)

0   1km

Old Tracks and Roads. *Drawn by WYAS.*

unfenced, unmetalled, tracks running through the ploughed fields of the township or across the heather and mosses of the commons and waste. Important ways led into the common fields; the plough teams of the village drove along Long Leading (Long Ridding) Lane, Southfield Lane (now Stockinger Lane), Back Lane and Bark Lane. Some of these have developed into modern roads, some remain only as footpaths and bridleways, (see Nesfield map (p. 15) which brings this out very clearly). Most of the old Roman road fell out of use, particularly the eastern end. The middle part, still called the Street, remains as a track and footpath and the western portion later became part of the turnpike system to Skipton.

Before the overwhelming importance of the wheeled vehicle no sensible traveller would think of walking or riding by Steeton to journey to Keighley when the packhorse tracks by Gatecroft and Windygate Nick saved so many miles. Nathaniel Johnstone mentions 'Sledgates about half a mile east of Wingates...Sledgates lyes in the road to Bingley and Bradforth'. These and other paths were often worn hollow and were cobbled in difficult places. Bridges were laid over the becks, a single stone as at Brigstone Close or a wooden log or a small bridge such as the one to the church known as Moorside Bridge. In the middle of the village, where the Main Street crossed the Town Beck, there must once have been a fairly difficult ford. This was bridged over before or during the seventeenth century for it was washed away in a flood in 1687 and rebuilt two years later at the expense of Staincliffe wapentake. On the other hand there was only a ford across the Town Beck in North Street until 1839 when this ford was considered dangerous and was bridged. The Wharfe had fords, a major one at Cocken End at the boundary with Ilkley, served by the track from Keighley going northwards and by the many tracks along both river banks and towards the wild moorlands to the north. The river itself was never suitable for boating save in small stretches. The Low Mill kept a row boat and possibly the rectory. For a time there was a ferry (later superseded by a footbridge) near the top of North Street.

The King's highway came from Otley through Ilkley towards Skipton and the north-west. This road was winding and inconvenient, nevertheless it was an important link between the east and west through the Aire Gap, as it had been used for centuries before. The road closely followed the river particularly where the high bluffs of the river bank allowed a fairly dry passage. It was not straightened or made easier until after the coming of the turnpike roads in the next century.

The repair of the roads and tracks was the responsibility of the township; each ratepayer was supposed to do four (later six) days a year unpaid work on the upkeep of the roads. Where there was an advantage to the farmer or the village it was done willingly but when a highway only served a few outlying farms the obligation to repair was much resented. Every twenty years or so one of the highways was allowed to get into such disrepair that the village was threatened with legal proceedings. Thus there was a threat in 1668. A much longer and more complicated case was brought at the Wetherby sessions in 1689 and later at the Knaresborough sessions. The road from Ilkley followed the river closely as anyone walking the present 'Dalesway' will know for they are following the mediaeval road. From Cocken End it went through woodland along the river bank before turning north through fields called 'Longholm' and 'Crookebanks alias Sandilands' (Sandbeds) towards the Smithy Greaves. The indictment stated 'by the violent trapped course of the river is much worn away'. The Justices, Henry Goodrick, Sir Walter Vavasour and Sir Jonothan Jennings heard that the highway was in disrepair 'about fifty rods was yet in great decay for want of repayre so that the King's and Queen's subjects with horses and carriages cannot travel without great danger of their lives and losses of their goods'.

Addingham pleaded that the former owners of the fields through which the highway ran had helped to build up the river banks and brought witnesses who testified that Samuel Wade, his son Thomas and Thomas' widow Rosamund had all helped to strengthen the river banks. These stated that the Wades had repaired the banks at their own costs; that they had made 'weares' (weirs) using great elm boards and wooden piles. Mrs. Rosamund Wade had hired workmen to fell and lead ryse (brushwood) to the waterside. The Wades had also allowed a little of their land to be used for the highway where the river had made a breach. Now, however, the land belonged to Sir Jonothan Jennings who would not allow any of his land to be taken into the road saying, 'if passengers wanted a way they might ride up the river'. We do not know the outcome of this trial, nor of the suit that Addingham brought against Sir Jonothan Jennings for not allowing land for the highway but, in 1690, the road was inspected by two Justices and considered to be in a satisfactory state.

The Quakers

Not far away in the western Pennines, on Pendle Hill, in 1652 George Fox had a vision. His followers became popularly known as Quakers. Despite very considerable persecution a number of families joined the Society of Friends. A few Addingham families became convinced Quakers. They were not the humble weavers and small farmers found in Lothersdale on the other side of the river Aire but seem to have been substantial farmers who built up estates of land. One family, that of Joshua Dawson, lived at Upper Gatecroft. There were at least three Dawsons in Addingham in 1612 but Joshua, born in 1615, seems to have been the only one to live on the Moorside. His three sons pre-deceased him and

Farfield Quaker Chapel, built by George Myers in 1689. Now in the care of The Historic Chapels Trust. *H. Holmes.*

his two daughters both also married Quakers; Deborah married John Lawson, a merchant of Lancaster, and Mary married Roger Coates of Kildwick. Joshua appears as a caring and compassionate person. When he served his year as Overseer of the Poor his accounts give the reasons for his payments and we see the human tragedies behind the bare accounts. Nothing is known of any business connections he may have had but during his life he built up a considerable agricultural estate. Joshua seems to have been an early convert. His house was licensed as a Quaker meeting house after the passing of the Toleration Act in 1689. After his death another Quaker family, the Hirds, came to live at Upper Gatecroft. Part of the farm was let to the Emmots, another Quaker family, who lived at Lower Gatecroft. The Hirds too were faithful Quakers. William, John and Thomas, three brothers, lived and farmed together. Only William married. His son seems to have moved to Leeds and a descendant William, doctor of physic, died there in 1782 leaving property in Addingham. The most important Quaker family in the district and the one to influence village affairs most was the Myers family. Anthony Myers was born in Beamsley, in the parish of Addingham, in 1619. He became agent at Bolton Abbey to the Countess of Cork and later to the second Earl of Burlington. He lived at Catgill then at Hesketh (both in Bolton Abbey). Together with Richard Smith he appeared in a list of recusants in 1665/6 by which time he had moved to Farfield. Here he provided a burial ground for the Society of Friends, in which, after the passing of the Toleration Act, he built a small meeting house. Anthony bought and lived at Farfield farm and also rented the larger Lobwood farm adjoining from the Earl of Burlington.

The inventory of his goods taken at the time of his death in 1698 shows that he lived in quite a large house with many rooms. They included a housebody, wash house, milk house and little parlour downstairs with five chambers above. Outside, in the stable, were a horse and harness; in the barn four cows with two stirks, two calves, one little calf. Also eight heifers 'letten forth'. He was in his seventy-ninth year when he died and may already have passed some farming responsibilities to his son.

Anthony had one son, George, who married Mary Hardcastle of Hardcastle Garth, daughter of a prominent Nidderdale Quaker family. His four daughters married Stephen Smith of Farfield, John Tennant of Langbar, Jno Baynes of Embsay and Matthew Lupton of Bradley. George Myers, his son, also a fervent Quaker, had attended an illegal meeting at Askwith and was sent to York gaol but as no evidence was offered against him he was released. Despite the strength of these prominent families not more than half a dozen followed in their footsteps. George Myers inherited house and farm from his father and as a landowner and a Quaker had an influence in the village which is best narrated later.

References

The 1611/12 Land survey. *WYJAS (Leeds)*. Accession 2161.

Vavasour Land Sales. *Deeds in private possession.*

The Constable's and Overseers Accounts. *WYJAS (Bradford)*
   Addingham Parish Council Records. 49D90.
   Addingham Church Records. 48D90.

R.Hoyle (ed.)., 1978. '*Lord Thanet's Benefaction to the Poor of Craven in 1685*'. *YAS, DD 121/88.*

Chapter 4

Farmhouse and Farm

Introduction

THREE hundred years ago the Main Street looked very different from the row of tightly packed houses we see today. As will be shown later nearly half the houses which then existed were not in the Main Street at all, but were scattered in the fields from the Moorside to Farfield, farmhouses standing in their own lands. The long Main Street from the Green at Townhead to Townend at the eastern end of the village had a scattering of houses and barns interspersed with crofts, greenfields and some cottages. The 1817 map shows that the village was still like this but by 1845 many of the crofts had been built on and the street had taken on its modern appearance.

We do not know the site of the original settlement. The 1585 map of Nesfield (p. 15), which shows part of Addingham, has drawings of closely knit houses along Church Street (originally called Kirkgate). The field in which the church stands, now called the Church Orchard, was part of the demesne lands of the Hall and the Manor. Both church and hall stood within it but it separated them from the village proper and the peasant houses which spread along Church Street to the lower end of the village. In Craven it is quite common for the church to be at some distance from the village houses. The stocks and pinfold were situated near the present Fleece Inn, another sign of the centre of village activities. At least one house on Church Street stands on mediaeval foundations (Fir Cottage) and nearer to the Main Street the West Yorkshire Archaeology Service identified part of a mediaeval farmyard.

The great rebuilding which swept the north of England in the 17th century removed and replaced the earlier houses. The mediaeval houses were timber built. The more important ones were probably of box frame construction, probably including the Hall and Plumtree Banks. The smaller buildings, houses, cottages and barns would be of 'cruck frame' (p. 47). In 1619 a deed mentions Robert Smith, housewright, who would certainly be erecting timber framed buildings. James Greene, glazier, of the same date would be putting small panes of glass into mullioned windows. Remnants of internal timber partitions are found in the Manor House and Upper Gatecroft. A mile away at West Hall in Nesfield the timber posts of a box framed house were later encased in stone, as also those in Hollin Hall towards Ilkley.

The simpler cruck framed houses would be thatched. Such a cottage was that repaired by the Overseers of the Poor for Ellen Taylor at Crossbank which was given a new 'ribb' (probably a cruck blade) and thatch (p. 34). Similar thatched houses remained in the adjoining villages of Storiths, Ilkley and Middleton until the latter part of the nineteenth century. The 'Sailor' Inn was a thatched house until 1838 when it was substantially replaced in stone. It is impossible to give certain dates for the stone buildings or rebuilding of the houses. Even the dates carved in stone on the farm lintels may indicate a marriage rather than a new building.

The reasons and method for rebuilding are well explained by a witness to a law suit (between 1699-1706) over leases made by tenants of the Ermysted School farms. Thomas Holdsworth, cooper, aged 61 years, gave evidence that he had known the farm (School Wood) for twenty years.

'...and remembered William Cockshott take down the greatest part of the dwelling house upon the said farm which was very much in decay and ready to fall down, and did rebuild the house in a very substantial manner and thatched the same with new slate and layd new chamber floors therein. The boards therein were bought by the said William Cockshott but the Aler (larch) wood and timber used in the rebuilding of the said house were either felled upon the ground or taken out of the wood and timber that was in the old house...'.

Many of the present farmhouses and buildings have re-used timbers as purlins or rafters, taken from former buildings on or near the site. Most of these timbers seem to have been parts of cruck framed buildings, the evidence being in the diagonal rebates made to fasten a collar or tie beam to hold the pair of crucks together (p. 47).

The Hearth Tax

A series of taxes were imposed in the mid-seventeenth century. All the house occupiers had to pay a yearly tax of 2s on each hearth, though the poor were exempted. The tax was unpopular and sometimes evaded (how did they conceal a hearth?) and was repealed later in the century.

The lists of taxpayers are extremely useful, first as giving the name of the occupier and the number of hearths in his house and, secondly, to compare with contemporary deeds, to find where a number of families lived and consequently it is possible to follow at least parts of the routes the tax collector took.

In 1672 the route started at the rectory where Mr. A. Kippax paid on two hearths, then Jonothan Jennings (at Plumtree Banks – he was the owner not the occupier) with three hearths followed by Mr. Ingram Frank (or Francis), innkeeper of the King's Arms, who also had three hearths. The collector then started at the east end of the Moorside and went westward calling at Gildersber, Small Banks, Crossbank, Whitewell and Sanfitt before returning to the Green where Grace Harrison lived. From the Green he presumably came down the Main Street though whether he called alternately at each side or went down one side and back up the other side it has been impossible to determine.

There were thirty-nine houses in the outlands and only thirty-four listed in the Main Street from Grace Harrison at the Green to John Green at Low House (the saw mill). The remaining fourteen houses were along Church Street on the way to Farfield where Anthony Myers' house had three hearths and one hearth at the mill. As has been mentioned the poor people were exempt from the tax and consequently not listed. Judging by the payments made to the poor by the Earl of Thanet a few years later (see p. 37) there could have been as many as twenty extra households on the Moorside and thirty more dwellings in the village.

Of the 133 hearths the main were in houses with a single hearth (54) and 25 houses had 2 hearths. Only 5 houses had 3 hearths, 2 with 4, and one, John Green's house, with 5. As far as it is possible to tell the inns had either 3 or 4 hearths.

The hearth tax was taken as the rebuilding of houses in stone was beginning. As the farmholds had been sold by the Vavasours fifty years earlier a class of freeholders had been created. They were able to do as they wished with their houses and, once the disturbances of the Civil War were over, the rebuilding started in earnest. John Green, with his five hearths, must have been an important person. He acted as agent for the remaining Vavasour lands and his house in Main Street was considered to be the Manor House (Speight, 1900). (This is not the original Manor House which fell into the river.) A fine cartouche in this house, now above an upstairs fireplace, is dated 1663. This was closely followed by Anthony Ward's single storey cottage (now the library) of 1669. Edward Clarkson, a tanner on the Moorside, rebuilt his house in 1670 and John (or possibly Joshua) Dawson rebuilt Fir Cottage in 1677. Henceforward a steady rebuilding took place, some with dated houses, but many with no dates. It is possible to give a rough date to houses as styles changed and some of the earlier arrangements were considered old-fashioned.

Building Developments

The earlier houses as discussed were either box frame or cruck built. Most barns were also cruck built and thatched. The old barns have completely disappeared, being rebuilt and enlarged during the agricultural expansion of the late eighteenth and early nineteenth centuries. Often the cruck components of the building were re-used in the roof trusses of the new barn. Traces of these can still be seen in barns such as Paradise Laithe, Low Brockabank and Throstle Nest. One barn at Small Banks has such a complete set of re-used timbers that it is possible to reconstruct its earlier phase (opposite). There are many others which have not been examined which would show similar evidence. These older barns were also thatched, even the barn at the rectory was thatched until it was rebuilt in 1806.

As farmhouses and cottages were rebuilt they did not copy the plans of the larger halls and manor houses of the gentry but simpler dwellings evolved which followed the preferences and convenience of the farmer in a style which we now refer to as 'vernacular'.

The oldest house in the village has already been mentioned. Fir Cottage has been altered many times since its mediaeval origins. (It is to be expected that the older the house the more often it will have been altered and the more complex its history.) The evidence for its mediaeval phase was found under its present floor when a stone hearth was discovered in the centre of the floor, a typical position for a mediaeval fire. The smoke was allowed to percolate through the thatch or through a hole in the roof ridge. This house was rebuilt in 1677 by J & M.D (either John or Joshua Dawson). It has been through many alterations since. The fireplace was moved to a transverse wall across the centre of the house and was moved again later.

Two other houses have signs of timber work within. The Manor House, built in the late sixteenth or very early seventeenth century, looks back to mediaeval arrangements. There are three main rooms; parlour to the west, central housebody in the middle and kitchen to the east. The kitchen and housebody each had a firehood against a transverse wall. Above the parlour was a 'great chamber' originally open to the roof as the decorative arch-braced truss, now concealed in the underdrawing, shows. This chamber was a relic of the mediaeval 'solar', an upstairs room to which the family could withdraw. The chambers have plank and muntin panelling and one of the kingpost trusses supporting the roof is filled with struts in an A-pattern, another relic of the timber frame tradition. The firehoods have been replaced – the one in the housebody with an early eighteenth century cantilevered stone arch with panelled jambs. The kitchen firehood was first replaced with a straight headed chimney piece At this time it might have covered four beehive bread ovens as four flues were found when it was altered. More recently this chimney piece was removed and replaced with a modern type.

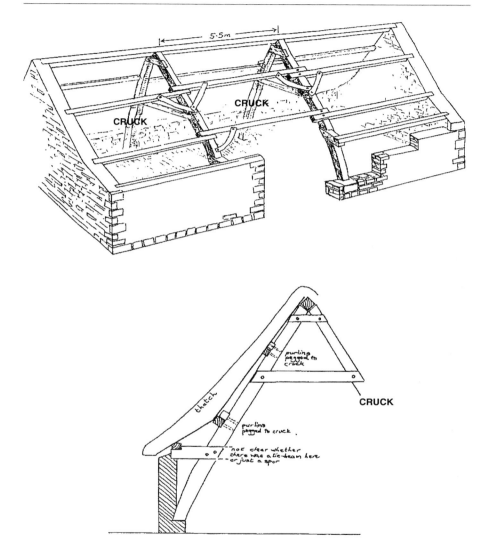

IVY HOUSE BARN, SMALLBANKS

This is the suggested reconstruction of an earlier barn on the site. The timbers drawn are all in the roof of the present barn with only wall plates and collars missing. The timbers making an 'A' are called crucks. Farmhouses, cottages and barns were usually built by this method until about 1660. *Surveyed by Alison Armstrong.*

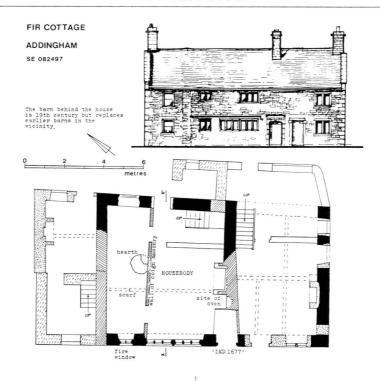

FIR COTTAGE

ADDINGHAM

SE 082497

The barn behind the house
is 19th century but replaces
earlier barns in the
vicinity.

0   2   4   6
metres

hearth

HOUSEBODY

scarf

UP

site of
oven

fire
window

'IMD 1677'

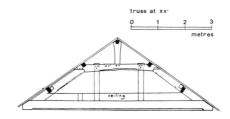

truss at xx'

0   1   2   3
metres

ceiling

N.B. Scales differ for each drawing.

FIR COTTAGE, CHURCH STREET.

Phase I. House with open hearth, probably timber framed. Two and a half bays. (Hearth stone found under the floor in 1988.)

Phase II. Insertion of upstairs floor with fire window to light a hearth under firehood on west gable. Walls rebuilt in stone 1677, marked black.

Phase III. Housebody altered, fire removed to east wall with false voussoir arch (hatched).

Phase IV. End bays converted into separate dwellings (about 1800).

Drawn by Malcolm Birdsall & Arnold Pacey.

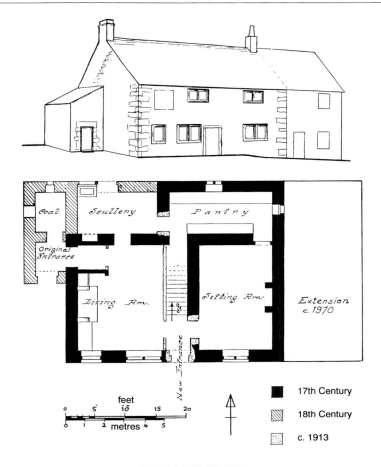

Legend:
- ■ 17th Century
- ▨ 18th Century
- ▦ c. 1913

OVERGATE CROFT

Phase I. A two-celled house with entry through a porch in the west gable. The fire would be under a hood and reached from the outer door around a screen with an upright post or heck to support a ceiling beam. The fire area lit by a 'fire window' on the south side. The sites of stairs and service room unknown but perhaps similar to Lumb Beck.

Phase II. Re-organised and extended rear premises (seen by changes in the masonry). About 1800 the firehood was replaced by an iron range. The rear rooms raised to two storeys and the roof raised.

Phase III. 1913. A central front door inserted on the south side leading to new stairs. Some mullions were removed from the windows.

Phase IV. An extra house built on the east end incorporating some rooms from the other house.

Plan supplied by John Milner, drawn by Arnold Pacey.

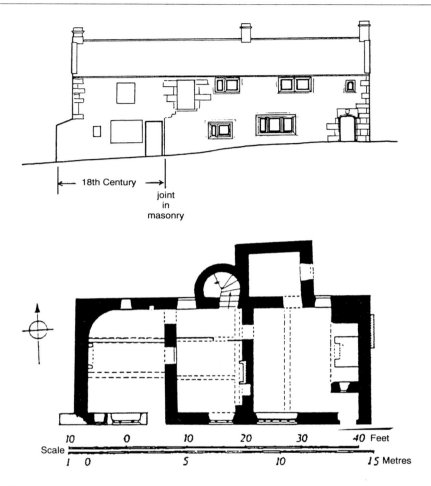

Plan © RCHM

LUMB BECK

Built by Edward and Susan Clarkson in 1670. Possibly a linear three-celled house from the beginning.
The fireplace is a very large arch of single shaped stones. A small internal window in the framework
of the side of the arch allows a little light in. Another internal fireplace, not in its original position,
was also dated. The newel staircase and a service room were in outshots at the back. The whole
house was demolished and re-erected to the same plan in 1970.
© *National Monuments Record. (RCHM).*

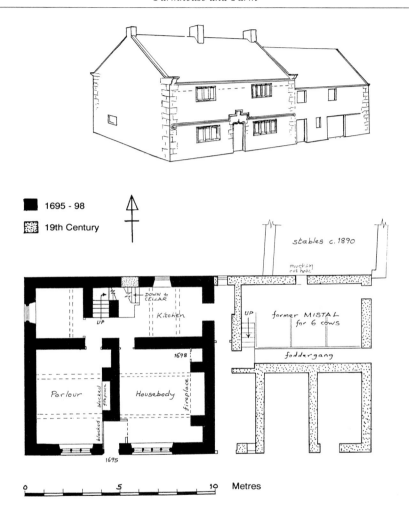

CRAGG HOUSE

A house built new in 1695 it was always one and a half rooms deep with a row of service rooms along the north side. There were two fires, the principal one on the east gable. A fine stone arched fireplace with a small oak doored spice cupboard at one side is dated 1698. The main door, with a handsome ogee head initialled and dated TAR (Thomas and Ann Rishworth) 1695, opens into a central lobby. Later the mullioned windows were lengthened and the roof was raised slightly.
Drawn by Arnold Pacey.

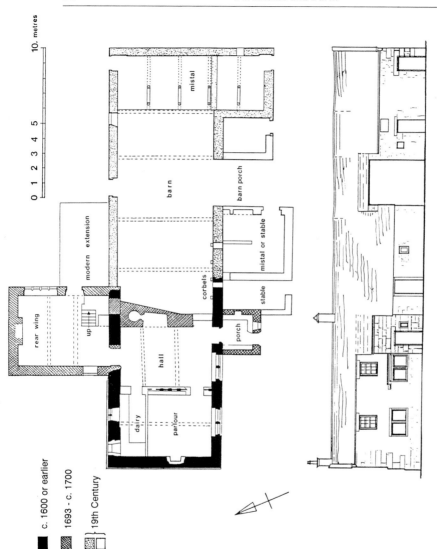

0 1 2 3 4 5   10. metres

UPPER GATECROFT

Another early house which has had many alterations. It probably began as a three-cell stone house quite early in the seventeenth century, with a wooden plank and muntin panelling between housebody and parlour. A partition divided front parlour from rear dairy. Phase II consisted of taking one room into the barn and a fireplace was built projecting into the barn incorporating a beehive oven. Phase III. A new kitchen was built to the rear with new entrance, datestone 169? and initials AHWH (Ann and William Hird). They may also have erected the porch in which it is said Quaker meetings were held. Later phases were mainly alterations and additions to the attached barn. *Drawn by Arnold Pacey.*

Another farmhouse with early features is Upper Gatecroft, Moorside. It seems to have been a simpler style than the Manor House. Probably originally of three cells (the eastern one later taken into the barn) with a plank and muntin partition between the housebody and the parlour, later replaced by a stone wall. Only the head beam with a slot to frame the panelling remains as evidence. A fireplace with an internal beehive oven was inserted when the third room was taken into the barn (opposite). A rear kitchen was built when the Hird family lived there from the 1690's. This new room obscured any former arrangements for a stair.

After stone became the favoured building material the hearth in the centre of the floor was moved to the wall and covered with a firehood which was supported on a horizontal beam (bressummer). These large fire areas were often lit by a small 'fire window'. No firehood has survived in a local house but the signs are there of their former existence. Because of the bressummer the spine beams in the ceiling, which were also supported by the bressummer, were shortened. After the bressummer was removed the spine beams were lengthened with short pieces using a diagonal (scarfed) joint. Houses such as the Manor House, already mentioned, Street Farm, Overgate Croft and Low Sanfitt all show this type of joint.

Overgate Croft was originally a two-celled, two storey house with a fire hood against the west gable. This gable had a lean-to porch which sheltered a gable entry to the house. The entry came round the post which supported the bressummer. There was probably a single storey service room at the rear and possibly a stair turret, though no trace of early stairs remain. Later the service room was extended along the whole length and raised to two storeys and at the same time the roof was raised making a house one and a half rooms deep. In 1913, the house was again remodelled. A central door and staircase were put in and there are even further alterations as each generation remodels its home to its own requirements.

The firehood had some obvious disadvantages and, later in the seventeenth century, another type of fireplace was introduced. These were constructed with handsome wide stone segmented arches. The stone, usually a fine gritstone, is nicely dressed and makes a handsome feature in the housebody. Such fireplaces had long been used in castles and superior dwellings but now came into the ordinary home. Lumb Beck (1670), Low Crossbank and Cragg House (1695) have similar arches.

By the end of the first quarter of the eighteenth century, instead of using separate stones to build the arch, two cantilevered stones were used supported centrally by a separate keystone. The two large stones were inscribed with lines to simulate individual stones and often have to be examined closely to determine whether they are true segmented arches or have false voussoirs (wedge-like stones). Houses with this type of fireplace are quite common. They are found in Low Brockabank (1728), Winebeck (1733), 5, The Green (1746), Small Banks (1749), Street House Farm, Holme House, Low Holme House, Sunbank, Lower Gatecroft, 112 Main Street and the Fleece Inn. The Fleece, where the hearth would have had a utilitarian purpose, has plain jambs but many of the others have jambs with raised panels. Later in the century fireplaces became smaller with flat mantelpieces and by 1800 the cast iron range was being introduced and the hearth was more confined.

The position of the principal entry was important. As well as Overgate Croft, School Wood also had a gable entry. More common was the direct entry as at the Manor House, Crossbank and Gildersber Cottage. The lobby entry was also common. Here the door opened into a lobby against an axial chimney stack as at Cragg House, High House, Moorside, and Low Brockabank. By the mid-eighteenth century changing fashions required a symmetrical house with a central door and rooms on either side. New houses were built to this plan and others were altered to try to achieve it. The most complete alteration took place at Low House whose door and windows were replaced, the windows with flat mullions. The date stone, with initials JG 1675, was removed to a rear door. The stone mullioned windows of the Manor House and High House, Moorside, were also replaced with the fashionable flat mullions and some of the windows were enlarged, though the entrances were not altered.

The three cell seventeenth century type of house has been mentioned. As it was only one room deep it was difficult to find a place for a staircase and service room. The problem was solved by making a stair turret at the rear with a newel (circular) staircase and a small outshut next to it as a service room. Lumb Beck and Street House farm are good examples. Gildersber and Crossbank Cottage have newel staircases and probably others have disappeared in later alterations.

Later the stairs and service room were joined and raised to two storeys along part of the rear, as at 112-114 Main Street, and, eventually, the narrow rear rooms were extended along the whole length of the house as at Cragg House, Low Brockabank and Winebeck making houses one and a half rooms deep. This seems to have been the common form of houses built after 1700.

The coarse sandstones and grits used for building did not work easily to make decorative features but doorheads with initials are very common. The ogee (S-shaped) doorhead is also used – the most handsome being Cragg House. By the mid-eighteenth century the design had become stylised and is found on a number of doorheads in the Main Street.

Internally, beehive shaped ovens are quite common. They would be built after

was frequently made (either wheaten bread or 'maslin', a mixture of wheat and rye). Potatoes appear in three lists, John Rishworth on the Moorside, Richard Shackleton at Small Banks and Ed. Popplewell at Beamsley, all between 1711 and 1720. Much later in the century tenancy agreements begin to mention turnips.

At the other end of the scale the poor people had few goods and left no wills. After they had been buried the Overseers of the Poor sold their remaining goods. A few lists of these sales survive in the township accounts. The poorest of all was Frances Wilkinson whose coat, shift and pettycoat made 5s.6d., two potts 6d., one wheel and stand 1s.6d., two coverlets and one rundlet (small barrel) 6d., one reel 7d.

Thomas Blakey in 1740 lived in a two-roomed house, 'in the house one chest, one cobert (cupboard), two desks, one chare, two tables, one backstone and a reccon. In the parlour one bed and bedding, one other pair of bedstocks and two chests' – no values are given.

Almost a third of Addingham inventories showed that the testators had money owing to them. It was often lent out at interest as bills and bonds. George Myers lent out about £1000 in this way. Similarly, as has been mentioned, Henry Harrison, the maltster, lent about £500. Most of the sums were quite small but, in the absence of banks, it was one way of circulating money, making money available to those who needed it, and solved the problem of keeping money in the house.

References

Ripon Historical Society, 1992. *The Hearth Tax List for Staincliffe and Ewecross Wapentakes* (Ripon)

Yorkshire Vernacular Buildings Group. *Reports on Addingham houses and barns.* YAS (Leeds)

Borthwick Institute of Historical Research. *The Wills and Inventories of Addingham* (York)

DATED HOUSES AND BARNS IN ADDINGHAM

Before 1700	Low House (cartouche), Crossend	JGS	1663	John Green
	Old School, Main Street	AW	1669	Anthony Ward
	Lumb Beck	ESC	1670	Edward Clarkson
	Sanfitt	WD	1671	
	Low House, Crossend	JG	1675	John Green
	Parkinson Fold (Fir Cottage)	JMD	1677	Dawson
	Friends Meeting House		1689	
	Cragg House	TAR	1695	Thomas and Ann Rishworth
	High House, Moorside	WCJC	1697	William Cockshott
	Cragg House cupboard	TJR	1698	Rishworth
1700-1750	Stone at Upper Gatecroft	TR	1712	Thomas Rishworth
	Gildersber	B?	1717	Bramley
	Low Brockabank	REL	1728	Richard and Elisabeth Lister
	High Bank Barn Main Street		1730	(does not belong to barn)
	114-116, Main Street	CJ	1730	
	Barn in Beever Close	RLE	1733	Lister
	Winebeck	TTE	1733	Thomas Topham
	Low Gatecroft		1743	
	5, The Green	HH	1746	Henry Harrison
	88, Main Street	CJM	1748	
	Small Banks (Lofthouse)	WL	1749	
1750-1800	High House, 156, Main Street	WBS	1752	William and Sarah Bland
	82, Main Street	JCM	1755	John and Mary Cockshott
	Brumfitt Hill	JBS	1755	Brumfitt
	Cuckoo Nest	TC	1758	Thomas Cockshott
	105, Main Street		1762	
	8, Main Street, near Craven Heifer	WSS	1766	
	136, Main Street, Crown Hotel	WDA	1769	
	Cottage (Bottom of Chapel St. demol)	WH	1771	
	Main Street, Manor House porch	RSM	1774	Richard and Mary Smith
	Small Banks barn	LWE	1776	William Lister
	Lister's barn, 99, Main Street	TLM	1777	Thos. & Martha Lister
	Street House barn	HLA	1779	Henry Lister
	Small Banks barn	RSS	1779	Shackleton
	Farfield Hall barn	JMM	1783	John and Mary Marsden
	Small Banks house	RSS	1785	Shackleton
	Peak Ridding		1786	
	High Bank, 46, Main Street	JCM	1790	John & Mary Cunliffe
	Daisy Hill	TLM	1797	
	8, Moor Lane	JE	1797	John England
	News Room, Chapel Street		1797	
1800-1820	Garth Cottage, 118, Main Street		1800	
	Saw Mill	AFM	1802	Antony Fentiman
	Tithe barn, Rectory	JCM	1806	John and Mary Coates
	Burnside	TCE	1811	Thomas Cockshott
	Bolton Road (demol)	WWS	1811	Wall
	144, Main Streeet	WWD	1812	Wall?
	High Mill Lane	HWM	1812	Wall?
	Street House barn (Side of door)		1816	Lister, Hargreaves
	Cockshott's Place, 38, Main Street	WC	1817	
	Peak Ridding garage	GC	1819	

Chapter 5

The Eighteenth Century

The Myers Family

GEORGE Myers, son of Anthony, inherited the property at Farfield on his father's death. He also took his place as agent of the Bolton Abbey estates and became a personal friend and mentor of the young 3rd Earl of Burlington whom he accompanied on his 'grand tour' of Europe. They returned in 1713 but he died shortly afterwards.

George (the elder) died a rich man leaving about £1000 in money and farm stock besides land and houses which he had been buying steadily. These properties were registered in the West Riding Deeds Registry (established in 1704) and are easy to trace. One of the most important of his purchases was Addingham corn mill which he bought from Reginald Heber of Hollin Hall; the Hebers and the Greens had owned the mill since the Vavasours had sold it in 1620.

The house in which George Myers lived at Farfield was very substantial. His inventory lists a three storey house including a low dining room and great dining room, a hall, three kitchens and at least eight chambers upstairs. The low closet contained books, frames and shelves worth £20. The best chamber, as well as bed, bedding and hangings, contained a carpin cloth (carpet), eleven chairs, two oval tables, eleven silver spoons and a silver can, glasses and a decanter. He also had eight maps, five guns, coffee pots, seeing glasses and a weather glass. George Myers had a son, also George, and a daughter Hannah. The younger George was still a minor when his father died but this did not prevent him from buying the manor of Addingham from the Vavasours. The manor and manorial rights included 120 acres of common, part being on the east and part on the west adjoining the lordship of Silsden. Also included was the millstone quarry and all other mines and quarries of coal, iron, stone, lead, copper, limestone and slate in the enclosed ground and outpastures and commons called Heathness, Newlands and Intacks. This deed was signed by Mary Myers, tutor and guardian of George Myers, the 29th & 30th June 1715. As the Myers were dedicated Quakers they did not buy the advowson of the church. This was leased to various bodies until

William Thompson bought the living in 1745. There was some friction between the lord of the manor and the rector during the whole of the century. George Myers at that time owned the field near the church known as the Church Orchard. He ploughed the field, including the footpath to the church, much to the distress of the congregation. These differences between squire and parson must have played their part in moulding the character of the village. It encouraged among the villagers an independence of mind and an ability to run their own affairs which is plain to be seen by reading the parish accounts and records.

The younger George Myers continued his father's policy of buying property, both cottages and land, although perhaps not as rapidly as before. In 1722 he married Elizabeth Laycock of Halifax commented on in *Dickenson's Marriage Register* as 'rich quakers'. George continued to serve the 3rd Earl of Burlington, though probably not full time. In 1728 he and Elizabeth built the present Farfield Hall around the earlier house. It is an important Grade I listed building described as 'Yorkshire Baroque'.

George died childless in 1739 and his property passed to his sister Hannah Chaytor. She too was childless and died three years later leaving her property to a distant cousin George Smith, an apothecary in Skipton. Another cousin, Ebenezer Jackson, challenged the inheritance and, as the Quakers did not go to law, they put it to arbitration. The award gave Farfield and the adjoining land to Ebenezer Jackson while George Smith took the lordship of the manor, the cornmill and some of the Addingham houses. Thus an estate which had been built up by purchase was divided owing to the failure of a direct heir – as had Joshua Dawson's estate been divided fifty years earlier. This happened again later in the century. When Jackson died unmarried his property passed to his nephew John Marsden (his initials and the date 1775 are on a barn in the farmyard of the hall). He too died without issue and his sister, Elizabeth Travis, inherited. She never lived at the hall. It was let to various tenants until she sold it in 1805.

The Church and Churchwardens' accounts

The Vavasours had held the advowson of the church – the right to present the living – ever since they were given the manor of Addingham after the Norman Conquest. They were a Roman Catholic family, held firmly to the old faith and were known as 'recusants' because of their refusal to conform to the Church of England. Eventually an Act was passed vesting such Catholic benefices in Cambridge and Oxford Universities. Robert Allot was appointed in 1714, presented by King's College, Cambridge. He resigned, being a non-resident, to be followed by James Carr AB, presented by the King. James Carr, from a

The Church, with the manorial fishpond in the foreground. *H. Holmes.*

Giggleswick family, was a 'pluralist' being also parson of Bolton Abbey and schoolmaster at Bolton-by-Bowland.

On the death of James Carr Cambridge University presented the Reverend William Thompson who then bought the living. The Thompson-Ashby family hold the patronage of the living. Mr J. Thompson-Ashby is now patron. The first William Thompson came when the Church of England was slack. John Wesley and his Methodist movement were about to sweep the country. Thompson seems to have been a vigorous man who instigated the repairs to the church (see below) once he had won the confidence of his parishioners. He does not seem to have persecuted the Methodists as some parsons did. Tom Illingworth of Scargill (whose diary will be quoted later) attended Church and then attended Methodist meetings and did not find them incompatible.

From the beginning of the eighteenth century the churchwardens' accounts are nearly complete. During the first part they are routine and concern mainly the running expenses of the church. This included the repair of the two bridges – the one known as 'the bridge in front of Elizabeth Frank's door' (later known as

Bryan's bridge) and the little bridge, called Moorside bridge, which people from the Moorside used. The churchwardens had other statutory duties, such as paying for fox and polecat heads, both of which appear in the accounts. One rather odd item appears in the 1650 accounts (one of the few surviving accounts of the seventeenth century). This is for 'destroying the picktors in the church'. These were Tudor, or Mediaeval, wall paintings on the south wall and chancel arch. They were whitewashed over but were faintly visible when Harry Speight wrote *Upper Wharfedale* in 1900. Now, alas, they are once more covered up.

A few secular occasions were celebrated. May 29th, 1686 was commemorated as 'King's day' when Elizabeth Frank was paid 2s for ale. On November 5th, the same year, 4s3d was spent on ale for the ringers, as also 'pouder plot' in 1752 when Brian Bailey received 7s6d. Mr. Beeston preached on Feast Sunday 1752, his entertainment cost 2s. The singers on Easter Day and December 25th were likewise refreshed. There is no mention of rushbearing in the accounts though Nathaniel Johnstone in 1669 had recorded that it took place on midsummer day.

When William Thompson bought the living of the church in 1745 it must have been obvious to a young and energetic parson that the church had been neglected and was badly in need of repair. He must have stirred the churchwardens into action. Robert Carr, a builder and father of the famous architect John Carr, was consulted about building a new, enlarged, church. His estimate of £1,135 must have shocked the parish deeply. There was no rich patron. Mr. Jackson at Farfield Hall and the Smiths, Lords of the Manor, were both Quakers. Relations between them and the rector were strained as the Quakers refused to pay tithes to the 'steeple houses' as they called them.

Yet the church must be repaired and it was decided to do it by direct labour. The story can be traced through the well-preserved and carefully prepared accounts for the years 1752-1760. To begin with the money to pay for the work must be raised. A deputation (Mr. Coates and Mr. Breare) went to Haworth to find out how to proceed to obtain a 'brief'. A brief was an official letter, approved by the Justices of the Peace, which was sent out to the churches in selected dioceses. The contents were read to the congregation who would respond by giving money to causes which they considered worthy. The brief was approved and endorsed at the Knaresborough sessions. The cost of travelling, obtaining a certificate and appointing trustees (Mr. Carr and Mr. Wilson, both of Skipton) was £4.1.3d. The brief was sent out and distributed in the Stafford area.

In 1756 3s. was spent at Brian's at the first meeting about the church. The churchwardens drew up contracts with various workmen. Hugh Spencer allowed stone to be taken from his quarry in Spencer's Gill (now Walker's Gill). The main contract was with Joshua Breare and Thomas Spencer, masons, who agreed

Farfield Hall, rebuilt by George Myers the younger in 1728. *H. Holmes.*

to rebuild the south wall of the nave, to be like Mr. Jackson's at Farfield Hall, 'with rustick corners three to the yard'; to make three new windows and to dress one new doorstead; to open Hugh Spencer's quarry for stone and to slake lime. There was a penalty if it was not completed by October 28th. They also agreed with Mr. Thompson to rebuild the chancel wall.

Thomas England and Thomas Guyer carried out the carpenter work. England arranged to prop the roof trusses and Guyer made a new loft (probably the gallery at the west end of the church). William Colburn of Otley agreed to glaze the windows and a number of other men contracted for other supplies. The chancel had to be finished by November 1st. This agreement was signed by two more masons, John Hargreaves and William Hustwick, as well as Joshua Breare and Thomas Spencer.

Preliminary work started on repairing and strengthening the approaches, the bridge and gates. Again ale was paid for at Brian's for the masons, 'when they wrought at bridge, each man a pint o' the day, 2s 4d.'

When the south wall was rebuilt there must have been an external south porch which was demolished. Nathaniel Johnstone, in his visit to the church in 1669, describes ancient stones in the wall of the porch. These were re-used in the lower courses of the tower. They were exposed briefly but have been covered with plaster once more. Perhaps they, together with the wall paintings, will one day be uncovered as witnesses to the fabric of the ancient church.

The tower itself does not seem to have been in the original plan. There was, appparently, no tower before the repair of the south wall. The agreement to build a 'steeple', as it was called in the contract between the churchwardens and the masons, is not dated but was part of the restoration. Formerly there seem to have been only two (or three) bells which were housed in a bell cote. The contract for building the tower specifies 'a steeple at the west end of the church taking in the west-end wall of the church for one side thereof'. Details of the measurement and style follow including a staircase with steps ten yards high, at four steps in a yard, with two old doorsteads setting in, one at the bottom and another at the top of the same.

Originally it was intended to send the old bells to York to be recast and a further one added making a ring of four. This was done but, when the bells were hung, there was dissatisfaction with their sound. The metal was not up to standard and the bells were taken down.

The churchwardens refused to pay for them and decided to order a peal of six new bells from Messrs. Lester and Pack of London (now the Whitechapel Bell Foundry), at the same time informing them of the dispute with the York bell-founders. Lester and Pack duly shipped the six bells and their clappers from London to Hull where they were transferred to a sloop upriver to Tadcaster. A carriage was sent there from Addingham to fetch them to the church.

The bells were hung under the supervision of Mr. James Harrison of Barrow in Lincolnshire. On September 8th, 1759 the *Leeds Intelligencer* reported 'This day was finished here (Addingham) by Mr. James Harrison in Lincolnshire the hanging of six bells from Lester & Pack, bell founders in Whitechapel, London. The next day was rung upon them, by a set of ringers from Otley, several peals, viz Oxford Trebles, Bob College, Pleasure College, Treble Bob and Crown Bob. The whole consisting of 2,530 changes performed in one hour and thirty-two minutes, to the great pleasure and satisfaction of the numerous concourse of people from different parts assembled on that occasion'.

The cost of rebuilding the south wall of the church and building the tower was £160. The Brief money collected eventually totalled £157 so the repairs were easily paid. Paying for the bells was a more difficult and complicated matter. There was a dispute with the York bellfounders about the bells supplied by them. These were eventually sent to Lester and Pack in London who paid for the metal leaving a deficit of £7 due to York which was duly paid off.

The bill for the six bells from London was £246.1.0 which was raised to £285.1.7 with the incidental expenses of transport, making the bell frames and hanging the bells. There were also still a few expenses connected with the fabric of the church so that by 1762 the total churchwardens' bill was £395.7.9. The money to pay off the debt was raised by increasing the church rate for 1759, 1760, 1761 and 1762 to £87 a year. The debt was not quite paid off and sittings in the newly installed pews were sold to as many families as would buy them. £30 was also borrowed from the capital of the Bulcock and Parkinson charity. This money had been left for the use of the poor of the village and the churchwardens paid interest of £1.10.0 yearly until about a hundred years later when compulsory church rates were abolished and the principal sum was lost.

This was the last major repair to the church although later records are sparse. Faculties are non-existent which should have been applied for when alterations were made. There were alterations during the nineteenth century when the chancel (which was the responsibiliy of the rector or patron) was repaired. The box pews were replaced with pine. An organ was installed and, at an unknown date, a clock was installed in the tower. One very urgent need was to enlarge the graveyard. An appeal was made for funds to buy the extra land from the adjoining landowner who demanded £100 for the half acre, claiming that it was valuable building land. The purchase was completed satisfactorily in 1868 and relieved the pressure on the old burial ground.

From Tracks to Turnpikes

In 1699 the manorial court for Kettlewelldale ordered the constable of Addingham to make and hang two gates at the Townhead, one at the narrow place near John Teale's house and another at the back of John Shaw's house and to make both to 'go and come well'. This was to prevent the cattle from coming off the common into the town and the fields. There was also a gate onto the common called the Flass Gate at the top of Cocken Lane.

The roads were no more than tracks maintained only by the unpaid labour of the ratepayers, which they called 'common day's work', on six days yearly. The local tracks and lanes would be maintained and even well looked after where they were in general use. Footbridges were laid over the becks and stiles were made in the walls but there were constant complaints by long distance travellers about the condition of the highways. The solution, finally found, was to make toll roads.

The turnpikes, as they were popularly known, started an era of much easier travel. For the first time many roads were reasonably well kept and easier to follow. The first turnpikes were not new roads but only existing highways which, by Act of Parliament, could charge a toll; this toll being theoretically sufficient to pay interest on the investors' money and to pay for necessary repairs. That the

Jeffrey's map of 1777

trustees had a duty to keep the roadway in repair did not absolve the townships through which it went from their statutory duties to maintain it.

This was well recognised by the inhabitants of Addingham when in 1755 an Act was proposed for turnpiking a road from Cocken End (on the boundary between Ilkley and Addingham) to Black Lane Ends near Colne. The road, though it did not compete in importance with the great Keighley to Kendal turnpike, nevertheless is fairly well documented and of considerable interest. The proposed and original line of the road is well shown on Jeffrey's map of 1777. Starting at Cocken End, at the junction with another newly formed turnpike from Leeds to Skipton, it went up Cocken Lane to what was then unenclosed moorland and then down Brown Bank to Silsden. Thus it did not go near Addingham village at all and was no advantage to it except for access to a few outlying farms.

The debate on the Bill explained why it was considered an advantage. It was said that woollen manufacture was carried out in Ilkley, Addingham and Kildwick parishes; that there were 300 or 400 weavers and many others employed under them; that the cloth was usually conveyed to Halifax and Colne on horseback; and that if the turnpike should take place from Kildwick to Leeds it would open communication through to Tadcaster; and that the poor weavers might join in a carriage for conveying their goods; also that the masters would find it easier to get their wool from Hull to Tadcaster and through Leeds to the part of the country where the manufacturers live.

The principal inhabitants in Addingham knew that the proposed turnpike was of no use to them and thirty of them combined to oppose the Bill in Parliament. They agreed to pay their costs by laying an assessment upon themselves, similar to other local assessments. As was to be expected they lost their case and the turnpike was duly set up. For many years it was known as Bawdwen's road as William Bawdwen of Stonegappe in Glusburn was a chief mover of the Act. Addingham inhabitants stuck to their guns and would not repair Cocken Lane and were duly indicted at York Assizes for not keeping in repair 'two thousand yards in length and eight yards in breadth'. A certificate issued by two of His Majesty's Justices in 1757 stated that it was well and sufficiently repaired.

By 1778 the road was once more in a bad state for 3,836 yards and the village was indicted at the Knaresborough Quarter Sessions 'so that the liege people of the Lord, now King, cannot go, travel or pass that way either on foot, horseback or with their coaches or carriages without great danger to the common nuisance of all the liege people'. From the evidence collected to defend this case it seems that the road had been in a dilapitated state a number of times and the officers of the village had been indicted on several occasions. The defendants stated that before the Turnpike Act 'the road was only a bridle road if any public road at all, no carriage could pass and scarce a horse'. They complained that the Commissioners of the turnpike took land to widen it without contracting with the owners and they had not paid for these lands. In 1734 the road had been indicted as a carriage road but the suit had failed and in 1735 it was indicted as a pack and prime way and they were fined £20. It appears that Addingham's grievances were genuine.

Another turnpike was made in the same year (1755). This was the toll road from Leeds to Skipton. It followed the ancient winding road along the river bank between Ilkley and Addingham. (This is now part of the long distance footpath called the Dalesway.) As one walks on the bluff above the river it is difficult to believe now that it was used by carts and carriages as a highway between Yorkshire and Lancashire. The two turnpikes parted at Cocken End as the road to Addingham closely followed the river bank, so carefully repaired by Thomas and Rosamund Wade a century before. The way passed through the Smithy Greaves, an industrial site, once a source of iron ore to be smelted on Smithy Hill. By this time Isaac Robinson was removing limestone pebbles from the river and burning them for quicklime in his limekilns. The road still followed the river along what was later called Low Mill Lane, although the Low Mill was not yet thought of. It wound its way past the rectory and the church before curving southward into the present Main Street. A branch veered to the north, possibly just a track, towards Bolton Bridge on the way to the northern dales.

The Skipton turnpike continued up the Main Street to Townhead and the Green, then to Moor Lane which was probably a remnant of the old Roman road to Ribchester. The road climbed the heights above Draughton continuing along the edge of Rombalds Moor to Short Bank descending abruptly towards Skipton. The poet Gray travelled over this road from Skipton to Addingham describing it as the worst road in all the country, he wrote 'first up Shode bank (Short Bank), the steepest hill I ever saw a road carried over in England for it mounts in a strait line without any other repose for the horses, than by placing stones every now and then behind the wheels, for a full mile, then the road goes on a level on the brow of this high hill over Rumbald Moor till it gently descends into Wharfdale ... and a beautiful vale it is, well wooded, well cultivated, well inhabited but with highways in the distance'.

Slowly the turnpikes were improved, some of the twists and turns were taken out. Obstacles were removed although the compulsory common day works were still continued. The bend in the road towards the Smithy Greaves was removed (no wonder it had been called Crookey Lane) and the highway was carried straight forward to the junction, going towards the church until it curved back into the

Main Street. The old road was sold back to Robinson for £8. The village people refused to mend this road further than the rectory gate. The final straightening (to 'New Road Top') did not take place until about 1835. Again there was a refusal to take responsibility for the road to the east of the village 'in its present state'.

There were two major diversions early in the nineteenth century. The old coach road to Skipton was re-made at a lower level through Draughton much to the relief of T.D.Whitaker who said that 'the terrific road over Rumblesmore which has appalled stouter travellers than Mr Gray will now be avoided by a diversion which, in the length of four miles, encounters a much smaller ascent than heretofore in one'. A few years later a new road was made to Silsden from Townhead through Cringles, a broader and safer way than the old Turner Lane or by the drove road to Silsden Moor – Parson's Lane.

When the new road to Silsden was made the old Cocken End road was dispiked and reverted once more to being a country lane. A bar house was placed at the top of Bloe (Blow) bank on the Leeds-Skipton and another one on the new Silsden Road where it crossed Turner Lane. This survived until 1954 when it was demolished to improve the sight line at the junction of the two roads.

The tolls charged in 1781 were:
> For every waggon or wain cart or other carriage drawn by six horses or beasts of draught the sum of two shillings
> Drawn by five or four horses or beasts of draught two shillings
> Drawn by three or two horses or beasts of draught one shilling and fourpence and drawn by one horse sixpence (except those going empty or laden with coals or lime)

The surveyors of the highways, like other village officials, were originally unpaid and held office for a year. By 1800 they were being paid small salaries and were also paying workmen for some work on the roads. Every use was made of local quarries. Some near the roadsides may have been opened purposely for providing stone for the roads – Paradise delf on Farfield Lane and Hunterlands on part of the common on the Silsden road were used. In 1783, 195 loads of stone were broken at Hunterlands. Bridges became more important and many becks were crossed by a log or a stone. Ale was given to the men for getting up the bridge where the Town Beck and Back Beck meet – once known as Capplegangs now, usually, as Aynholme bridge. This bridge is narrow today, but consider its condition as late as 1905 when the *Craven Herald* reported that the council surveyor had been staking out a piece of land belonging to the Lord of the Manor, adjoining Aynholme Bridge, 'which is to be thrown into the road there. It will take off a very awkward corner, the land is a gift to the authority and will average twelve feet and in places sixteen feet wide'.

Many of the present stone bridges were designed by the West Riding surveyor Bernard Hartley who worked from 1797 – 1855. The style of stonework which he used with very characteristic horizontal tooling gives even the smallest bridges elegance and is as good as a signature of his work. The Wharfe was never bridged at Addingham; there was a ford by the corn mill and one at Cocken End. The Beamsley parishioners came to church by ferry. A boat house is mentioned in 1781. The ferry was worked by the Robinson and the Norris families until a wire footbridge replaced it in 1892.

We have already seen (Chapter III) that there were inns in the village in the seventeenth century. Elizabeth Frank, Robert Cowan, Jane Hodgson, Ellen Stott, Thos Mayson, Robert Parkinson and Thomas Bilborough were listed as alehouse keepers in 1689. Elizabeth Frank, widow of Ingram Frank (or Francis), kept the house at the corner of Church Street and North Street at the entrance to the access to the church. It would catch those who had reason to use the church – the churchwardens often held their meetings there – and the travellers also found it a good resting place. After the death of Ingram Frank in 1679/80 Elizabeth, his widow, continued to keep the inn until her death in 1704. Her inventory of March 1704 shows that the inn was comfortable and well stocked. There were salt meat and oatmeal in the house, wheat and oats in the barn, swine, cows and heifers also in the barn. Seven beds accommodated travellers with linen worth £3 and pewter also worth £3. Later, Brian Bailey took it over and it became known as the King's Arms. After the turnpike was finally altered and the line diverted to New Road Top in the 1830's the King's Arms lost its licence and is now a private house.

Ellen Stott, another of the innkeepers, lived at the top of the village in what was probably a predecessor of the Craven Heifer. She died just before Elizabeth Frank. Later in the century William Spencer kept the Fleece, which may also have been a seventeenth century inn, and William Bramley had an inn at the top of the village. Later, in the earlier nineteenth century, Marmaduke Spencer was at the King's Arms and Richard Wall at the Fleece. John Fentiman kept the Crown, with John Cockshott at a mysterious house called the Glowworm, perhaps a predecessor of the Sailor.

Mills and Millstones

In its long history, first mentioned in 1315, the corn mill has been altered and rebuilt many times. The weir slanting across the river is in part one of the oldest mediaeval constructions in the village. It must have been washed away many times but, once established, the site would remain the same. The mill and adjoining land were sold by the Vavasours in their land sale of 1619 to John Greene of Addingham and, in 1713, George Myers bought it together with the adjoining ten acres of land. In this deed it is described as an 'ancient water corn mill now two mills (perhaps meaning two waterwheels) and a farmhouse adjoining thereto … and a building near the mill called Addingham Kilne with all kilne hairs etc. for £640'. The account books for the mill and the kiln survive for this purchase year 1713/14.

The kiln book records small payments for 'sive' (sieve) and fan presumably for winnowing the corn. Further payments were made for sacks which must have been for drying the grain before grinding. The mill book for the same period seems to record many small sales to different customers from half a peck to four pecks (4 pecks to the bushel; a measure of volume of 8 gallons). The main sales were for 'shilling' which were probably shelled crushed oats rather like a coarse oatmeal or groats. A few entries were for 'maselgin' – mixed corn, usually wheat and barley, occasionally for wheat or for 'moulter'. Although there is much detail in the books it is quite difficult now to understand exactly what the transactions meant.

During the long life of the mill many dates were punched into the stonework from the early 1600's onwards. Unfortunately most are now covered in concrete. The ownership passed from Myers to Smith until the death of Richard Smith the younger in 1794 after which it was sold. Richard's father kept a diary in 1776-7 in which he described the destruction of the weir after a period of deep frost in 1776; its repair in the summer; and its destruction from a similar cause in the winter of 1777.

Within ten years sites were being sought in the Pennines where the new textile machines – Arkwright's water frames – could be installed. All the water corn mills were used in this way. Richard Smith, hard on the heels of John Cunliffe, built a new textile mill for spinning worsted yarn. It was adjacent to the corn mill and worked by the same water wheel that drove the grinding stones of the corn mill, which were still in use.

Corn mills need millstones and these were made all over the Pennines where the stone was of suitable quality. The escarpment of the Addingham Edge Grit – part of the Millstone Grit series – makes a bold feature along the northern edge of Rombalds Moor, which was open and unenclosed. The Edge shows signs of quarrying along most of its length, although who quarried the rock, for what purpose and at what period, is not recorded excepting for the millstone quarry known as Millstone Lumps. This extends south-east from the Slade. It is now part of Silsden as the result of a demarcation made at the enclosure of Silsden Moor in 1773 but it was formerly in Addingham.

The first mention of the Millstone Quarry seems to be 1650 when the receipt of rent for the quarry is entered in the accounts of the Overseers of the Poor. An explanation of how and why the quarry came into the hands of the Overseers was given in a court case on the disputed ownership in the 1780's. 'The former Lord of the Manor of Addingham sold certaine shares of the commons to the freeholders of Addingham reserving to himself several things and amongst them the rest of 120 acres of common adjoining the outlines of Silsden but did not reserve the great stones therefore the freeholders let the millstone quarry and applied the rent for the use of the poor'. Although there is no rent recorded until 1650 the quarry could have started any time after 1618. It is even possible that the Vavasours themselves had allowed quarrying before the sale of their lands in 1619.

The Millstone Lumps consist of a triangular area reaching to the top of the escarpment (see map p. 126). The ground is rough and criss-crossed with sledge tracks. Towards the east are many large boulders but they were cleared from the west end as they were dressed and sold. In the middle a band of half-worked stone remains. Hollows in the ground together with small chippings of stone show where the stones have been removed. Coal ashes indicate that there was a forge in which the chisels and tools used for dressing were sharpened.

At least four leases for the quarry survive, made by the freeholders, with John Wainman. The first is dated 1685 leasing 'all that Cragg rock or quarry of stone commonly called Wingate Nick Cragg and full and free liberty to digg for break cutt and hew stones therein for millstones ... so far as the manor should extend'. The lease was for eleven years at £6 a year to be paid in two equal portions. For every pair of stones above sixteen got in any one year he had to pay a further 6s8d. He also had liberty to remove worked stones after the end of the lease, but not more than ten pairs.

Another lease of 1712 was made, again with John Wainman, on the same terms except that he could make eighteen pairs yearly. Later lessees were John Wade, John Teale and George Spencer. Spencer was still the lessee in 1787 when Richard Smith, then Lord of the Manor, started proceedings against the freeholders claiming that the quarry and the rent were rightfully his. Richard Smith was able to prove that Sir Walter Vavasour had left the quarry to his wife Dame Jane in his will dated 1695; also that in 1713 the quarry was mentioned in a legal document. The freeholders lost their case but petitioned Richard Smith to pay the rent to support the poor rate as had been done heretofore.

For many years Silsden had been in dispute with Addingham over the ownership of the millstone quarry. The boundary was ill-defined and each township claimed the same land. The agent for the Skipton Castle estate (which owned the lordship of Silsden) constantly pushed forward claims to the quarry even in 1757 drawing a map showing such farms as Scargill and the Slade on Addingham Moorside as being on the Silsden side of the boundary. The dispute came to a head in 1773 when the moors and commons of Silsden were enclosed. At this time Heelis was agent for Lord Hothfield of Skipton Castle. He arranged to ride the boundaries of Silsden with the commissioners for enclosure. These were ridden as Heelis wanted. When Richard Smith of Addingham heard that the boundaries were being ridden he joined the party and challenged the line being taken. He was reassured by Heelis that they would meet and agree together. The notice for objections was pinned up on Kildwick parish church door as was legally required. Unfortunately Richard Smith did not make objections within the allotted time. The parliamentary bill went ahead. New boundary stones and fences were erected. The Addingham freeholders pulled down the fences and trespassed in the new closes, for which they were prosecuted. The Addingham freeholders challenged the demarcation line in the courts. They lost their case on the grounds that they had been out of time with their objections and the boundary remained as ridden leaving Wingate Nick millstone quarry in Silsden. By this time the quarry was in decline. Millstones made from harder rock in France and Germany were both better wearing and shed less grit into the grist. This made them more popular with millers and consumers alike. Even so, in 1797, it was recorded that two grey stones had arrived from Addingham at Bainbridge Mill in Wensleydale. As late as 1830 Paul Pickard was listed as a millstone manufacturer (*Directory of Leeds and Clothing District*, Parson and White). He may have worked an area below the little Nick belonging to Lumb Beck (or Gill House?) farm in which there are also a number of half-worked millstones, gateposts and stone troughs.

Consider the length of time the quarry was in work – at least 150 years (1650-1800) – possibly longer, producing between 32 and 36 millstones yearly; that is between 4800 and 5400 in all. There are many half-finished millstones still on the hillside which probably developed faults during the dressing process and had to be abandoned, although some seem to have been perfect. The methods used in the dressing can be seen. First the rough stone was tilted and propped by smaller stones inserted beneath, then a circle was drawn and shaped. The flat top was dressed and the central hole cut. The stone was then turned over and the lower surface finished.

We do not know how the stones were moved. Perhaps it was on small, stout, stone 'sleds' which are listed in some inventories or perhaps slung under the axle of a pair of wheels. The 1757 map of Rombalds Moor shows three parallel tracks along the moor top; the middle one is labelled the millstone way to Otley. These roads were all closed after the Silsden Moor enclosure.

Of the men who wrought these stones, of their working conditions and how they were organised we know nothing. It was probably a young man's labour and as they grew older they might drift away into easier work. Not one man named in the Addingham Parish Register is described as a millstone getter. John Wainman was described as a mason. Their only memorial is the area cleared of stone and the half-finished stones abandoned on the rough slopes, together with the chance survival of leases and documents pertaining to the disputed ownership.

The Methodists

In the seventeenth century the Quakers had been the chief non-conformists but they were a declining group and inward looking. In the eighteenth century the teachings of John Wesley and his followers caught the attention of the weavers and textile workers of the West Riding. Tom Lee (p. 79) was one such person, eventually becoming one of Wesley's preachers, but there were throngs of such men and women who gathered at the cloth markets of Bradford and Leeds and passed the word on from one to another about gatherings and prayer meetings over a wide area.

The Illingworth family who lived at Scargill on the Moorside were a family similar to that of Tom Lee. They too were farmer-weavers living on a small, high, farm near to the boundary with Silsden. Tom Illingworth was about twenty-five years old when, in 1755, he began to keep his diary. He still lived at home though, shortly afterwards, he moved out to keep a school in Silsden. There were times when he helped on the farm at home – he records haymaking, bracken gathering, ploughing, potato planting and shearing (reaping) corn. He could also weave for later on he set up a pair of looms in his school. He tells of visiting his father at home and sitting spinning with him in the evening but more often he took cloth into Bradford on Thursday mornings. To catch the market he had to be up and on his way with horse and cart by 2.0 a.m.

Once at Bradford he often went on to a prayer meeting – his mother's relations lived in the Birstall area and he visited meetings there. His diary tells much of his doubts and heart searchings and these religious preachings were the most important parts of his life. He still professed himself a member of the Church of England and attended their services on Sundays, often going on to the Methodist preachers – the Reverend William Grimshaw, Thomas Colbeck, Jonathan Maskew and, on at least one occasion, John Wesley himself. There were class meetings at Addingham on Friday evenings, also at Silsden and other places, sometimes just at a farm house. The custom of meeting at a farmhouse on Addingham Moorside continued until the 1950's.

The Illingworths were only one family among many who wished to follow the Methodist way. By 1778 there was sufficient support to buy land and build a small plain chapel in what was then called Lidget Lane. The congregation grew and the chapel was enlarged in 1808 and again in 1834. For a time Addingham was head of the circuit.

Tom Illingworth travelled to London but returned to Keighley where he died in 1772. He did not live to see the changes which started to take place before the end of the century. Technical developments in the production of cotton textiles were taking place in Lancashire which revolutionised the textile industry and which will be recounted in the next chapter.

Schooling

An endowed grammar school was founded in Skipton in 1548. Ilkley followed in 1637 with another small grammar school. No record exists of the founding of a school in Addingham and no endowment was ever made. There is an enigmatic mention in the Constable's accounts for a 'dominie' (schoolmaster) in 1630. No other entries occur in the accounts until 1724. It is obvious from looking through the various accounts in the seventeenth century that quite a number of men were able to write (some barely legible, others with a good hand) so possibly there was a school for which no record remains. There is a building in the village always known as the 'Old School'. This started as a two-room single storey cottage built by Anthony Ward (A.W. 1669 over the door). His daughter, Sarah Green, wife of John Green, inherited it and we must presume it was bought by the village for use as a school.

During the eighteenth century a number of schoolmasters are named; John Butler in 1724, then J. Becket, schoolmaster, witnessed indentures in 1738. In 1750 the son of John Boocock, schoolmaster, was buried. In 1776 John Fieldhouse, the parish clerk, died suddenly and it was agreed to combine the offices of schoolmaster and parish clerk. By 1773 the teacher was William Parkinson Waterhouse who left shortly afterwards to teach at Calverley. An entry in the Town (minute) Book for the same year records that William Bell offered himself as master but the inhabitants agreed that his conduct was such as to make him unfit to teach and refused to elect him. They agreed to ask John Greenwood as long as he didn't put himself forward. William Parkinson Waterhouse was again offered the post in 1784 on the resignation of John Garlic. He refused to come back to teach but seems to have kept in contact with the village as both he and his wife were buried in Addingham.

The Old School. This was built as a single storey cottage by Anthony Ward in 1669 & later served as a village school until the end of the nineteenth century. *H. Holmes.*

The school fabric was maintained by the village – accounts for minor repairs are common. The Town Book (1690-1744) had a memorandum that it was agreed that the present schoolmaster be allowed £3 a year. He also received 15s for keeping the town's books and, presumably, the rest of his salary was paid in fees by pupils. He must have made a living by charging fees. Unfortunately there are no hints as to the subjects taught. With no endowments there were no regulations or rules. The school continued to be supervised by the township into the next century until it became inadequate for the growing population.

Another method of dealing with children was to apprentice them to a trade. These children lived in with their master's family and served for seven years after which they would be considered able to earn their own living and to have learned a trade. It was a method, supposedly, of seeing that poor children were privately maintained and were not a charge on the parish. The Best children were orphaned in 1742; their parents were buried on the same day. They were maintained by the Overseers who paid for 'Best' lass for a pair of shoes, two smocks, two approns, a pair of stays, a yard of Wolsey for a petycoat, two caps and a handkerchief in preparation for her apprenticeship. 'Best' lad needed two yards of cloth for shirts, thread and making costing 3s. A pair of clogs cost 1s1d and he was also provided with a leather apron and overbody (was he apprenticed to a blacksmith?).

Apprenticeship was a rough and ready method of bringing together increasingly unwilling masters and servants. Some of the youngsters were badly treated but not all were so unlucky. Tom Lee was born in 1727 near Keighley and when his mother died four years later he went to live with her brother in Addingham. He was apprenticed in Addingham 'to one in the worsted trade and was by a a kind providence placed in a family where I wanted for nothing that was needful either for body or soul'. So he wrote in his autobiography in *'Lives of the Early Methodist Preachers'*.

There were the usual unruly and mischievous boys and girls. The parish clerk recorded in the Town Book that he was to see if John Whitaker junior could be apprenticed to the captain of some ship. The application must have been unsuccessful for John Whitaker was put out apprentice to William Spencer later on that year. The situation seems to have become even more desperate and a letter was sent to Hull to see if places could be obtained on any of his Majesty's ships for a number of boys whose 'felonious actions have rendered themselves obnoxious and dangerous to the whole parish so that people are in danger both of their lives and properties'. With that recommendation no place was forthcoming. It was also agreed that if such application failed then they should be prosecuted at the expense of the parish. In fact another boy, John West, was prosecuted and imprisoned at York.

Farming

Agriculture too was changing. The small farms no longer sustained the farming families – now they were weavers, woolcombers or worked in other trades. The agricultural revolution of the lowlands had little place in the acid soils of the uplands. It was enclosing walling, liming and draining which led to the improvement in grass swards and stock carrying capacity. This allowed improved breeds of cattle and sheep to infiltrate the hilly lands. There are many miles of stone drains still working which help to dry the pastures, meadow and arable ground.

Such an improvement was made by Henry Harrison who lived on the Green. He kept accounts for improving 'Ruf Intack' between 1786-1790. He paid 1s6d

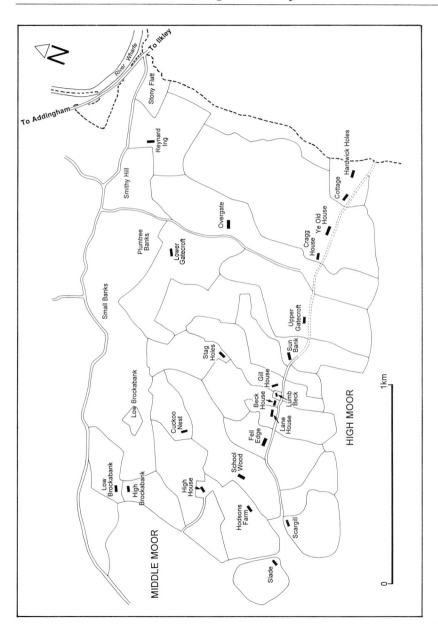

Moorside drawn from the tithe commutation map of 1845. *Drawn by WYAS.*

a rood (seven yards) for walling and an extra 1s6d a day for getting stones. Lime was brought from Draughton only three miles away; in all 259 packhorse loads at 9d a load. Stone drains were laid using sow (sough) stones. William and Joseph Holdsworth were paid 3d a rood for opening 121 roods of drains. The whole improvement cost about £15. No more information is given about the field which was probably at the side of Turner Lane.

The moors and commons – High Moor, Middle Moor and Low Moor were owned by the Lord of the Manor subject to the rights of the freeholders and farmers to graze stock and remove peat and turf. Much of the peat on the moor must have been stripped by the eighteenth century because inhabitants were forbidden to cut turf on the Low Moor. The gates across the lanes to the commons were also in disrepair for cattle strayed into the Main Street. It was ordered too that pigs must be rung to prevent them from rooting in the soils of gardens and crofts. The pinfold at the bottom of Stockinger Lane must have been well used for impounding straying stock.

The open fields of the village were gradually consolidated and enclosed during the seventeenth and eighteenth centuries; also the stinted pastures excepting Heathness. A proposal to enclose the moors was put forward by thirteen freeholders. For some reason they did not proceed further and the final enclosure did not take place until 1873.

Growth and Change

The population of old Addingham is difficult to estimate. 89 houses paid the hearth tax in 1672. Taking an average family size of 4.5 persons (assuming that there may be older members who have left home) there may have been about 400 people living in the hearth tax houses. The exempt poor must be added to this figure. The Earl of Thanet's charity of 1685 is very specific about the number of people benefiting and we find 135 people living in 57 houses. This gives an average of 2.4 persons per household which is considerably smaller than the multiplier of 4.5 used above. The smaller family size found in the charity lists is probably due to a greater proportion of aged or older men and women living alone. There is also a problem that a few of these houses may have been in the hearth tax list. The 135 people receiving the charity added to the 400 estimated from the hearth tax list comes to 535, a figure to be taken cautiously, but it does not seem unreasonable.

In 1743 the Archbishop of York, Archbishop Herring, visited all the parishes in his province. Prior to his visitation he sent a questionnaire to the parishes including a question on how many families attended church (which was compulsory) and how many dissenting families there were. There were 100 families in the congregation with only five or six dissenting families. The total again comes to about 500 people so it appears that there was no growth in population for at least seventy years. It is known that in this period the number of baptisms exceeded the number of burials. The likeliest explanation of the shortfall is that men left the village in search of work.

In the second half of the century there was a complete reversal and the population began to grow rapidly. This growth was partly through natural increase and partly through immigration into the village as evidenced by new surnames found in the Parish Registers. What attracted men to Addingham? Firstly, there were small plots of land on which cheap houses could be built. This was in complete contrast to the adjacent villages of Ilkley and Bolton Abbey, each of which was under the control of a large estate (the Middletons owned most of Ilkley and the Dukes of Devonshire owned Bolton Abbey). These two estates did not allow extra houses to be built and their population could not expand.

Secondly, a new branch of the textile industry was expanding rapidly in the West Riding. The weaving of worsted cloth by hand loom weavers in their own homes was becoming common, although a certain amount of linen was also processed particularly by the Cockshott family who, during the beginning of the next century, turned their expertise to worsteds and more particularly to cotton weaving.

Thirdly, communications had markedly improved with the provision of turnpike roads and, by diversions and straightening the line, they were made even better.

There were disadvantages in this population growth. More people meant more in need of relief and larger poor rates which were still raised on the land. How this problem was dealt with is shown in the next chapter (p. 90).

The newcomers were mostly textile workers – hand loom weavers in particular though, increasingly, as the worsted trade expanded we find more woolcombers. Often the small farmers also carried out woolcombing or weaving as a 'dual economy' with subsistence farming. An occupational analysis taken from the Addingham Parish Register shows the increase in textile workers very clearly.

Occupational entries in Addingham Parish Register (men)
(Percentages based on Pickles, 1976)

Dates	Land	Landless Labour	Textiles	Other
1767-80	25%	16%	24%	35%
1801-12	19.5%	4%	52%	24.5%

The worsted manufacture was organised by wool staplers. These men travelled to the East Riding and the Midland Shires to buy the long wools necessary for making worsted cloth. They organised the combing and the washing of the wool by the hand woolcombers who usually collected a cartload of raw wool, took it home to process, and returned a proportionate weight of combed wool known as 'tops'. The next process was spinning and agents carried wool far up the dales to the women who spun the yarn. This was then returned and sold to the hand loom weavers who wove their 'piece' of cloth and took it, as Tom Illingworth did, to market to be sold.

The worsted process, though simpler than making woollen cloth, needed a considerable amount of available capital to finance all the stages of manufacture. Spinning was the bottleneck and it was estimated that six to ten hand spinners were needed to keep one weaver supplied with yarn. Improvements in hand weaving due to the invention of the flying shuttle made the situation worse.

John Cunliffe of an Ilkley family, a grazier and woolstapler, married Mary Thompson, daughter of the rector, 'a young lady of considerable accomplishments and a fortune of £2,000' and settled in Addingham. John was of course aware of the difficulties of manufacture so was interested in the new technical improvements in spinning taking place in Lancashire. He went into partnership with John Cockshott whose family had been associated with flax and linen. Together they bought a small plot of land at Smithy Greaves in 1787 and built a mill of four storeys together with a dam across the river to feed the waterwheel which powered the mill. Although the intention had been to spin cotton they experimented successfully with worsted yarn using Arkwright's water frame. Ellis Cunliffe (John's son) was the first who took 'water twist' into the Bradford market. (Water twist was yarn spun or twisted by water power.)

Richard Smith with partners including Robert Hargreaves, a member of the worsted committee, built a new mill, next to the corn mill, in 1787-88 and also mastered worsted spinning. Ambrose Dean, using the beck at Town Head, and Anthony Fentiman both built small cotton spinning mills. These four mills provided work in the village well into the twentieth century.

(The story of textiles in Addingham is recounted in more detail in *Woolcombers, Worsteds and Watermills*. Mason, 1989.)

References

Hodgson, H.R., 1933. 'Myers and Farfield Hall'. *BA.*, NS Vol.5.
Addingham Churchwardens' Accounts. *WYJAS* (Bradford), 48D90.
Toynbee, P. and Whibley, L., 1971. '*The correspondence of Thomas Gray*', Vol.3. (Oxford)

Whitaker, T.D., 1812. '*The History and Antiquities of the Deanery of Craven*'. 2nd ed. (London)

Smith of Addingham. 'Addingham Mill Book'. *YAS*. DD 61.

Preston, W.E., 1952. 'Addingham Millstone Quarry'. *BA.*, NS Vol.7.

Parson and White, 1830. '*Directory of Leeds and Clothing District*'. (Leeds)

The Diary of Tom Illingworth. Typescript in Keighley Library, Local History Collection.

Raistrick, A., 1973. '*Industrial Archaeology*'. (St. Albans)

Ollard & Walker, 1929. Archbishop Herring's Visitation. *YASR*, LXXV,pt.3 (Leeds)

Pickles, M., 1976. In Local Population Studies, no.16.

Mason, K.M., 1989. '*Woolcombers, Worsteds and Watermills*'. (Addingham)

Alehouse Keepers, 1689. *YAS*, MD44, bundle D.

Chapter 6

The Industrial Village

The Cunliffes and Thompsons

JOHN and Mary Cunliffe settled in Addingham and raised a large family of four sons and five daughters. They probably lived in an old house at High Bank which they rebuilt; the datestone says JCM 1790. The house, in the height of fashion, was double fronted with large bay windows. Ellis, their eldest son, married Ruth Myers, heiress of the Manningham Listers, with a fortune of £30,000. She died in 1796 of consumption. Ellis had settled in Bradford and married, for his second wife, Mary Kay. He inherited the Lister fortune and added Lister to his surname. He prospered and invested in the Bradford trade. His fourth son, Samuel Cunliffe-Lister, became one of the great entrepreneurs of the textile trade later in the century.

In 1805 William Cunliffe, John's second son, bought Farfield Hall with its land and other property in the village from the Travis family – eventual heirs of the Myers. At the time of the purchase William Langton rented Farfield Hall. William Cunliffe appears to have lived the life of a country gentleman and to have taken no part in business life. He became a deputy Lord Lieutenant of the West Riding

A sketch of the old Parsonage House & a new Barn adjoining at Addingham

The seventeenth century Rectory. The crack in the gable shows how it was moving towards the river as had the Hall over two hundred years earlier. It was demolished in 1809, when a new one was built. © *Borthwick Institute for Historical Research.*

and a Justice of the Peace. William never married and after his death in 1823 his property was divided amongst his brothers and sisters.

Mary, John's eldest daughter, married John Coates the rector. Through her grandfather, parson William Thompson, she inherited the advowson of the church and became patron of the living which has remained in the family ever since. The other sisters all married. They all moved away from the village excepting Harriet who married John Ellis who built and lived at High House in the Main Street and later built Hallcroft. The various members of the Cunliffe family owned about 760 acres of land in Addingham as well as a large number of cottages and were the largest landowners during most of the nineteenth century.

Woolcombers and Looms

Throughout the nineteenth century the Cunliffes and their descendants kept their interests in the textile trade in Addingham. There were many difficulties to be overcome during the development of the mills and John Cunliffe encountered some of these business problems. One of his partners, John Cockshott, became bankrupt but the mill was saved probably with the help of other members of the Cunliffe family. After John's death the mill was let to a firm called Pullan who continued worsted spinning.

In 1825 Jeremiah Horsfall took the mill on a twenty-five year lease and came to live in Farfield Hall. He commenced cotton spinning and started to re-equip the mill. The following year it was attacked by a mob of machine breakers from Lancashire who erroneously thought that power driven looms were to be installed. They were chased away when the military arrived and Horsfall continued a policy of expansion (described in *Woolcombers, Worsteds and Watermills*, Mason, 1989). He built a new, larger, mill next to the 'old end', installed a steam engine, manufactured gas to light the mill and started a school for the factory children.

We know little of the working of the other three mills (the High Mill, Townhead Mill and Fentiman's) although Stephen Binns, once an overlooker at Fentiman's, gave evidence of the overworking of children to the Parliamentary enquiry of 1835. Different types of yarn were spun – cotton, linen and worsted. Partnerships were formed and dissolved. Some firms went bankrupt but to some extent all the mills carried on working.

The mechanization of worsted spinning led to a greater demand for the long-stapled wool suitable for weaving worsted cloth. This wool needed combing, a slow and tedious process of drawing out the long fibres of the wool parallel (these were called 'tops'). As demand for tops increased many were attracted into hand-combing which for some years was a well paid trade. Many of the small farmers

The Tudor organization of yearly appointments of unpaid officers – Constables, Overseers of the Poor, and Surveyors of the Highways – was no longer adequate. Men were unwilling to stand for office even when small payments were offered. Lists of men were drawn up from whom Officers were chosen by Justices of the Peace. In 1835 a 'select vestry' was formed. The first list for this included the chief landowners: Henry Alcock Bramley (Highfield), John Coates (Rector), Thomas Lister Thompson Cunliffe (youngest son of John), John Ellis (High House, husband of Harriet Cunliffe), four manufacturers, the surgeon Joseph Duckworth and three farmers. These 'select vestries' tended to be self perpetuating; on the death or resignation of one member another was co-opted.

The strains and stresses of the old method of poor law support had become intolerable. The Poor Law Reform Act of 1834 created Poor Law Unions which combined a large number of townships administered by a Board of Guardians. Addingham became part of the Skipton Union which served forty-nine townships from Buckden in the north to Cononley in the south and Addingham in the east to Elslack in the west. This arrangement survived until the Local Government Act of 1929 dissolved the Boards of Guardians and replaced them with Rural District Councils.

The new Unions erected Workhouses; the Skipton Union Workhouse was built on Gargrave Road in Skipton in 1839/40 and opened in 1841. The poor, unable to support themselves or feeble through old age, together with children whose parents could not look after them and some others, were placed in these Workhouses, often far from their old homes.

Overseers of the Poor were still appointed yearly: they still looked after houses owned by the village and let to the poor until pressure was put to sell their cottages.

Many records and accounts cease after the founding of the Select Vestry although there were a few town meetings at which matters important to the village were discussed.

Baines Directory of 1822 gives a glimpse of village life. Directories were selective with a bias to the more affluent. They show very well the types of tradesmen working and also the manufacturers. Farmers are also well listed. It must be remembered that the lists are not necessarily a complete compilation of all inhabitants.

There was a wide spread of tradesmen as may be expected in a growing village. Saddler, Whitesmith, Tallow Chandler, Plumber, Druggist, Cornmiller, Ironmonger, two Blacksmiths, Butchers, Bakers, Carpenters, Confectioners, Grocers, Drapers, Shoemakers, Wheelwrights and at least seven Stonemasons all worked in the village. Although Shoemakers are listed in the *Directory* Clogmakers, or Cloggers, were still plying their centuries old trade. Richard Smith records in his diary, in rather contrived doggerel, his appreciation of one of the members of this craft, probably too humble to be included in the *Directory*:-

> 'To ease your feet of cramp and pain
> John Stead's begun to clog again
> John Stead he thinks these clogs will do
> There's room for foot and stocken too
> If hasty clogging will invite
> Bring work at morn, it's done at night.'

Doubtless the Mills and new houses needed the services of these skilled workers. In these early years our village had more shops than Ilkley and many Ilkley residents came to Addingham to buy goods.

It is perhaps surprising that other industry has not established itself in the redundant industrial buildings or on other sites. There was a flurry of excitement at the beginning of the century when a small seam of coal was found in the Millstone Grits of Gildersber. It was thought what a good thing for Addingham it would be if a coal mine was developed. Fortunately for Wharfedale the coal seam was very small, as those are which occur in the grits. A small field, now built on and called Ridley's Fold, used to be called Coal Pit Close after an earlier discovery reported in the *Addingham Iris* in June 1845, 'We are glad to state that the efforts to obtain coal in the neighbourhood continue unabated. The workmen have now reached a depth of 17 yards, six of which are gravel, nine of shale and two of blue grit. An engine of eight horsepower and pipes of six inches bore are constantly at work. The spirited proprietors are very sanguine and we most heartily wish them success. Coal, and especially good coal, would be of great importance in this locality'.

Other early trades were tanning and malting. The Topham family were tanners, first near the now Memorial Hall and later at Winebeck. The Listers of Street House Farm, who had been candlemakers in the Main Street, were also tanners. The malt kiln has a history of at least two hundred years, William and Jno Wall owned it in 1817, it still belonged to the Wall family when it closed in the 1920's. It was not the only malt kiln in the village, there was one near the Craven Heifer, probably associated with an earlier Inn on the site.

There were also two surgeons and two academies. The academies disappeared before 1830 but the two surgeons were replaced by a Dr. Duckworth and later his two sons who practised in the village for many years.

Mrs. Gaskell described an incident in the Main Street when she and her husband were driving through to Haworth to collect material for her *Life of Charlotte Bronte*. A boy had fallen into the beck onto a heap of broken glass and had cut himself badly. The Gaskells rescued him and eventually found the doctor whose son managed to staunch the bleeding.

A further worry was the threat of cholera. It was suggested that a Board of Health should be formed. Ten men were appointed and they were allowed £15 for expenses. No cases occurred in the village until fifteen years later when a vagrant died of it and infected one other person.

The workers in the mills, as was usual in the early days of the Industrial Revolution, were mainly children and young people. Rickard's report of 1835-6 shows that this was particularly true of the worsted industry

Age	<10	10-12	12-14	14-16	16-18	18-20	20+	Total
Worsted	–	9	43	28	10	5	18	113
Cotton	4	13	42	38	41	35	85	271
Bland, Ellis	–	6	6	4	2	1	6	21
Totals	4	28	91	70	53	41	109	405

It was suggested that the women married in their earlier twenties and stopped working as they started childbearing. Many other children doubtless helped the weavers at home. A few went to school but there was little provision until the Church School was built in 1845.

Even with long working hours and working days the villagers looked at the wider world. One particular achievement, which must have affected the whole village, was the raising and sending to the House of Lords a petition to abolish the slave trade. This petition, although undated, refers to the cessation of the (Napoleonic) wars. It was started by the Reverend John Coates and was signed by well over 600 men. Unfortunately the bottom part of the petition has been wet and possibly eight or nine rows of signatures have been washed out.

A Friendly Society was started about 1800. The rules were rather restrictive but it was a safety net against injury and disease for those in early manhood and of childbearing age. The early presidents were the various millowners and employers of labour in the village who seem to have kept a prudent eye on the accounts. When the Society was wound up in 1845 (probably because many men had left the village in search of work) there was a good balance in the bank (£842) for distribution among the members. By this time national Friendly Societies such as the Oddfellows were taking over.

In 1842 a Mechanics Institute was formed with the aim of self help and education. Three years after its foundation the *Addingham Iris* or *Addingham Mechanics Institute Observer* was published monthly for a year until the editor left the village. The Institute held its second annual soiree on February 4th, 1845 at the Oddfellows

Hall where 200 people sat down to tea. It was announced that there were 69 members and that they had 225 volumes of books. Nothing is recorded of its early activities but, although no classes seem to have been organised, there were lectures and discussions. Meetings were held, as they were later, in an empty weaving loft over Garth Cottage. By 1884 it was described in *Craven's Directory* as having over 1,000 volumes of books and a news room supplied with local, weekly and daily papers.

Nonconformists

The Quakers were a declining group. Infertility in the two main Quaker families and lack of recruitment of new members seem to have been the chief reasons. The congregation slowly dwindled; there are records of meetings cancelled because of snow and the meeting first removed from Farfield to a room in Addingham. Later it joined the Ilkley meeting. Mary Smith, daughter of Richard Smith, Lord of the Manor, eloped with a Quaker farmer, John Emmott of Gatecroft. They eventually returned to Addingham but their family seems not to have belonged to the Quaker community.

In the meantime other denominations were flourishing. The Wesleyan Chapel had to be enlarged. Independent Row below Townhead Mill was so called because the top house had an upstairs room used as an Independent Chapel. This chapel never became firmly established and closed after a few years. The Primitive Methodists were more successful. They started by holding open air meetings, usually at the mills, and from the fervour of their meetings were often called 'Ranters'. They were closely associated with the Oddfellows. In 1838 when the St.Michael Lodge, No.249 of the Manchester Unity of Independent Oddfellows, built a hall on Lodge Hill a chapel room for the Primitive Methodists was included in the building. This also included four cottages the rent of which would bring income into its coffers. They remained with the Oddfellows until the end of the century when they built a new chapel by the Main Sreet (now the Memorial Hall).

The Mount Hermon chapel was built in 1861 with a Sunday School room below and the chapel above. Their congregation thrived also with faithful support from local families. Each denomination had its own Sunday School with its anniversary meetings and other religious and social occasions; for these occasions did revolve very much around the church and chapel. Choirs were formed and musical evenings were enjoyed. The Mount Hermon choir was invited to sing with massed choirs at Crystal Palace – an occasion for which they were very proud.

The Mechanics Institute. *H. Holmes.*

The Hungry Forties: bad times at the mill.

The years between 1840 and 1850 came to be called the Hungry Forties with good reason for work was scarce and badly paid.

The 1841 census returns showed a sharp fall in the population of Addingham which had been growing steadily for more than fifty years. The census returns explained this as due to the sudden closure of a large mill. In fact Jeremiah Horsfall had become bankrupt and the mill had ceased working. Horsfall left the country and it was conjectured went abroad for he was seen many years later near Waterloo by Jack Holmes of Addingham, a famous huntsman, who was hunting with a pack of hounds nearby.

Many people left Addingham in search of work elsewhere. The Overseers of the Poor made lists of empty houses and warehouses. This was also the period of successful mechanisation of weaving so the handloom weavers were suffering too. During this ten years the operation of the four mills is uncertain; some may have been empty for a while or working at reduced capacity. We know that the Low Mill was leased by Wm.Threlfall and his brother-in-law James Seed. Threlfall together with his sons was very much involved in the linen trade in Washburndale. He must always have been struggling and his reputation as an employer was not good. Eventually he too became bankrupt.

Besides having a large number of empty houses upon which no rates were paid, the Vestry recognised that some of the poorer families were unable to pay and they were excused paying the highway rate and in 1840 some thirty-five people were excused paying the poor rate.

Despite the poverty and difficulties of this time progress was made in some issues. Farmers were relieved of paying tithes in kind by the tithe apportionment of 1843. The church and chapels seem to have been thriving. William Greenwood, of Netherwood, bought a croft adjacent to the Wesleyan Chapel and presented it for use as a graveyard. When he died he was buried in a mausoleum in the centre of the yard.

The Projected Railway

The roads were much improved by the nineteenth century. Canals too had opened up trade; as the Leeds-Liverpool canal was only over the hill in Airedale and brought heavy goods such as coal and corn to be carried cheaply. The new type of transport, the railway, became all the rage. The railway fever which gripped the country in the mid-nineteenth century did not pass Wharfedale by.

The first Airedale line from Leeds/Bradford to Skipton opened in 1847. The nearest station to Addingham was Steeton about four miles away. There were proposals for other lines which came to nothing. A consortium suggested a railway from Colne to Addingham. *The East Yorkshire Airedale extension* was proposed in 1845. Although the main support came from Lancashire businessmen it was also supported by Bradford and Aire Valley manufacturers and businessmen. It was registered provisionally with a capital of £250,000 in 12,500 shares of £20 each; deposit £2.2.5 per share.

The projected railway was intended to supply the only link required to complete the chain of communications between the port of Hull, the manufacturing towns of Leeds, Bradford, Otley and Keighley and the manufacturing districts of north-east Lancashire and the port of Fleetwood. The subscription list included many people from the Colne/Clitheroe area. From Addingham Wm.Lister, tallow chandler, Wm.Smith, manufacturer, James Whitaker, engineer and Wm. Cockshott, draper, supported it.

An attempt was made as early as 1845 to estimate the amount of goods and the number of passengers who might use this projected railway. From November 1st to 14th a census of goods and traffic was taken at Silsden station (sic). In that fortnight 482 foot passengers passed on their way to Addingham, 156 horses and riders, 167 single horse carriages, 32 two to four-horse carriages, 103 oxen and 19 pigs. An average of 30 cartloads of merchandise a day (one ton per load) also passed through. This was mainly coal though stone carts and loads of wool, flax and yarn also went through nearly every day.

The Addingham manufacturers were also asked to estimate what they would be receiving and sending (see *Worsteds, Woolcombers and Watermills*), Threlfall's (soon to become bankrupt) being by far the largest potential customer. Of the others Wm. Lister, candlemaker, estimated 100 tons per annum of tallow from Bradford.

The company was dissolved six months later (perhaps as a result of these censuses) but the proposal was not finally abandoned until 1920. The scheme was said to have swallowed up £65,770 'and not a sod was cut'. The route proposed from Colne with a tunnel through to Lothersdale and another to Crosshills seems to have been utterly impracticable.

The railway arrived from Leeds to Ilkley in 1865. Both Ilkley and Steeton stations were much used by any inhabitants within reach. A number of people walked to Steeton station to catch the train to Keighley. Among them Job Brear from the Sawmills who went to the Grammar School in Keighley. The workers at Townhead Mill were taken by wagonette to Steeton and on by train to Morecambe on the occasion of the millowner's marriage. Carriers also did a good trade.

New Mills, New Fabrics

We have already seen that Samuel Cunliffe-Lister had patented and made successfully a machine wool comb from which he was making a large fortune. At this time (about 1850) after the bankruptcy of Threlfall at the Low Mill it was empty once more. Samuel rented it from his cousins and started working there. It is not clear which branch of manufacturing was carried on but soon Samuel had a new project in view. He had bought a large quantity of waste and gummy Chassam-Indian silk lying in a London warehouse. No-one had been able to extract and spin the silk from all the rubbish and Samuel determined to process it.

It took much money, patience and time to solve the problems. Samuel took a partner called Warburton – he lived at Holme House in Addingham for a while – and must have been experimenting at the Low Mill. Warburton eventually lost confidence and thought that the problems would never be solved. Samuel bought him out for £50,000 and continued alone. He eventually solved all the problems and started to spin combed silk extracted from the waste, making a product equal to silk from perfect cocoons. By 1871 the mill was busy spinning silk.

At the same time Lister was experimenting with mechanical velvet looms. Velvet is a double pile cloth. The pile was cut by hand by skilled velvet cutters who used special knives. The loom was perfected with the help of a Spaniard, J.Reixach, who was taken into partnership by Lister and it was working successfully by 1868. The patent of that year states 'Velvet cutting, two pile fabrics woven together face to face and are cut asunder by a knife which severs the pile between them'. The secret lay in the sharpening of the knives by revolving stones.

About this time the Cunliffe-Listers briefly came back to Farfield Hall to live before they bought and moved to new estates at Swinton near Masham. The census enumerator had difficulty in classifying Samuel and compromised by describing him as a 'gentleman in business'. At this time he had six children. Also living in were a footman, two nurses, a governess, a French governess, a housekeeper and seven maids. Samuel could well have been trying the new machinery at Addingham for there were well over a hundred silk operatives there in 1871 compared with the dozen or so of 1861.

Listers took over the High Mill and started silk spinning there also. A Scotsman, William Watson, came to manage the Low Mill. His son built another mill for silk spinning which, as a true Scot, he called Burnside. This later became part of the Lister group and the Watson family continued as managers and managing directors at Manningham and Addingham for nearly a hundred years.

After the revival of the textile trade in the second half of the century the population began to increase once more

1801	1811	1821	1831	1841	1851	1861	1871	1881	1891	1901
1157	1471	1570	2179	1753	1558	1859	1838	2163	2225	2144

By 1881 it had again reached the numbers found in 1831 but this became a plateau and numbers stayed more or less the same.

Improvements

At the same time improvements were being made to the services. These made the village a more comfortable and pleasant place to live in. Gas had been made at the Low Mill since before 1840. It was later taken to the village and supplied by the Addingham Gas Light Co. The gas was said to be too pure to use with gas mantles and was used as a naked flame. Gas street lighting was started in 1877. Mr.Hiley was appointed lamplighter at 30s. a week. Lamps were not lit on moonlit nights.

Procession down the Main Street possibly on the occasion of Queen Victoria's diamond jubilee.
H. Holmes.

Water for drinking had been drawn from town wells. One in Stockinger Lane was reputed to heal sore eyes. Another town well was (and still is) in the garden of one of the railway cottages. There were also wells near the cricket field and the top of the village but these were away from the houses. Doubtless the town beck was used for ordinary purposes.

The 1861 census return shows that a number of waterworks labourers were lodging in the village, who were working on the Barden aqueduct. Bradford was bringing water from new reservoirs at Barden to supply the city. The conduit passed under Chelker reservoir, through Addingham Low Moor and by Marchup to Cringles on its way to Bradford. Because the aqueduct passed through Addingham land the village was provided with water from the Barden supply. For many years this came through the Addingham Water Company. Later when Bradford brought further supplies of water from Nidderdale these aqueducts also passed nearby.

A 'tippler' sewage system was installed. Doubtless a great improvement on the middens and earlier methods of waste disposal. Land at the Sandbeds was bought in 1894 to make a sewage filter bed. This was superseded in the 1950's when Addingham was connected to the Ilkley sewage system.

Social life revolved mainly around Church, Chapel and Clubs. St.Peter's parish church had its feast day though the midsummer rushbearing mentioned by Nathaniel Johnstone had long died out. The Chapels held their anniversaries and the Clubs held a club day in September. The Oddfellows, Ancient Order of Buffaloes and the Foresters marched down the main Street with brass bands in procession and later dispersed to various public houses for a dinner and refreshment – a custom still carried out today on Gala Day. The Addingham brass band practised in the old house on Stamp Hill which became known as 't band 'oil'.

There was a cattle and sheep fair (later two) held behind the Swan and Craven Heifer Inns when up to a thousand sheep were for sale. Besides the livestock there were roundabouts and stalls. Dances, meetings and whist drives were held in various rooms – schoolrooms and empty rooms (perhaps earlier used for brewing) behind the Inns. The Oddfellows Hall was used for showing magic lantern slides and, for a short time, as a cinema. Cricket, Football and Rugby teams were formed and the Cricket and Football clubs still run successfully.

Old School, New School.

In the first quarter of the nineteeth century the changes and stresses of the expanding village were considerable. The school was a small, two room, single storey building which was erected as a cottage in 1669 and seems to have been adequate for the needs of the eighteenth century. In 1805 the Town Meeting (the equivalent of the Parish Council Annual Meeting of today) decided to raise it by another storey. After the rebuilding (which may have been from the foundations) the school was transferred to the upper room and the lower floor was divided into two to be used as cottages for the poor. In 1827 it was decided to make the western cottage into a lock-up or gaol. For a time the other room was used as a girls' school. The upper room was used as a school (latterly for infants) until it was closed at the end of the century. Later the lower rooms had a number of uses. Cottages for the poor, shops and a barber, Horsman (known as 'Waffy' to distinguish him from another Horsman family known as 'Toslem'). The Conservative Club used one room until a new clubhouse was built (now the British Legion Club). Now the lower room houses the Library and the upper floor is the Parish Room.

The provision of schooling had been the cause for some concern. The old school was quite inadequate for the number of children now in the village.

Jeremiah Horsfall's factory school had been discontinued although Threlfall allowed the schoolroom to be used as a Sunday School and there were one or two small private schools.

The rector, William Thompson, applied to the *National Society for promoting the Education of the Poor in the Principles of the Established Church* for a grant to help to erect a new school. He estimated the whole cost, including a house for the master, at £611 of which he had promises of £176; the probable grant was to be £250. There is no indication of how the shortfall in money was made up. The building was on glebe land at the west side of North Street and was to be of two rooms, one accommodating 125 boys and the other 125 girls. Later information says there was accommodation for 248 children and that there was no house for the master.

The *Addingham Iris* reported that on Christmas Day, 1845, the new school connected with the Church of England was duly opened. The scholars were treated to new milk and Christmas cake and the teachers with a public tea. '...the custom which has so long prevailed of regaling the scholars with beer has been substituted by a more wholesome regulation'. After tea the scholars were examined in geography. The Wesleyans held their annual missionary meeting and the Primitive Methodists had a public tea meeting on the same day.

The Wesleyans seem to have started a Sunday School, sometimes used as a day school in a house in Back Lane from the 1830's onward. Information about it is scanty but we can see that there has been a continuous desire to provide a basic schooling for children. The strains of the growing and changing population, coupled with changes in the administration of various functions in the village, seem to have led to muddles and even confusion (see p. 102). When the Elementary Education Act was passed in 1870 the situation changed. Inspectors decided that the premises in Back Lane were unsuitable and could not easily be improved. Two circuit ministers together with other members of the Chapel decided to press ahead with fundraising to build a new school for both Sunday and weekday use. £608 was quickly raised by gift subscription and efforts in the village. A plot of land was available and was bought near the chapel and building began. The new Sunday School was opened in July, 1873 and was visited by the Reverend Henry Flesher Bland, an Addingham man who had settled as a preacher in Canada.

The next year the day school was opened. The full time children paid 3d. a week and the half-timers 2d. until the abolishment of 'school pence' in 1891 when a fee grant of ten shillings per head was allowed although complete abolition of fees was not achieved until 1918. *(The 1870 Act only made compulsory the provision of school places although it allowed School Boards to frame by-laws to make school attendance compulsory. It was not until Mundella's Act of 1880 that school attendance became nationally compulsory and the complete abolition of school fees was not achieved until Fisher's Education Act of 1918.)*

Numbers grew rapidly from 23 boys and 23 girls in the early days to 240 when the two original classroooms must have been bursting at the seams. A new classroom was added in 1890 into which the infants moved which gave more space. Mr. Harry Hewerdine, still remembered in the village, was appointed headmaster in 1885 and stayed until 1924.

In the meantime there were questions about the status of the 'Old School' where, it will be remembered, there had been an infants' school. This was taught latterly by a Mrs. M. Lister, of the old Ilkley family of Beanland and wife of the carrier, until the infants moved into the Wesleyan school.

The Charity Commission was travelling the country enquiring into all the known charities. The enquiry into the Addingham charities took place in the Mount Hermon schoolroom on June 14th, 1894. After enquiring into other charities the ownership of the Old School was raised. The Rector and Churchwardens claimed ownership as the building and school had been managed by the Rector and his father, the Rector before him, for a hundred years. But a group of Methodists and the Methodist minister claimed that it belonged to the township and showed entries in the town book to prove it.

The evidence showed that during most of the nineteenth century the Rectors had appointed the schoolmasters, let the lower rooms and kept the building in repair and applied any money derived from it to support the church Sunday School. How the administration had come into the hands of the Rector was not explained but it was probably due to the default of the parish officers, particularly after the Select Vestry was instituted. The Methodists contended that if the township owned the building it was subject to educational trusts and that the income from it should be for the benefit of all the inhabitants alike.

There were two different traditions about the property:

1. It was left by some donor for the education of the children.

2. Left in trust for the poor supported by entries in the Town books.

The Charity Commissioners drew up a scheme in 1897 making it an educational charity. The scheme said that four trustees owned the buildings and profits but were bound by the charity to benefit children who were bona fide residents of Addingham. They could assist pupils to attend schools, institutions or classes for purposes of education other than elementary, to pay fees, travelling expenses or maintenance allowances and to attend to the health or physical condition of children attending. Otherwise promoting the education, including social and physical training, of boys and girls from the poorer classes, could be part of its work. This last was an amendment of the 1897 scheme that was introduced in 1936. The residual income was to be divided between the Church School (also known as the National School) and the somewhat larger Wesleyan School (see table on p. 118), and they received about £5 each.

The scheme came to be out of date after the re-organization (see next chapter) under the Education Act 1944. After the infants vacated the old schoolroom it was used (as it had been by the Rector) for various meetings. The upper room was rented to the Parish Council for £9 per annum. When the railway was being constructed it was used as a navvies mission room. It was suggested that the expenses of courses in horticulture and agriculture be paid for and the expenses of lectures in gardening and buttermaking were allowed. Another year there were classes in dressmaking, bent iron work and arithmetic.

Enclosure

The High, Low and Middle Moors of Addingham were open and unenclosed. The High Moor to the south was an extension of Ilkley Moor, part of the greater Rombald's Moor. The Low Moor was an area between the Silsden boundary on Counter Hill coming down to Town Head. The Middle Moor lay between Cocken Lane and Turner Lane as it goes towards Silsden.

The earlier urge to enclose by assarting or intaking had ceased after the Vavasour land sales of 1618-20. The commons were regulated by the Manor court but, by the end of the eighteenth century, the Township officers seem to have taken over their management. They appointed William Spencer as By-Law man and said that no-one had to grave (dig) turves on the Low Moor except for thatching and, the following year, even that was forbidden. In 1790 thirteen freeholders met and adjourned to John Slater's to consider what methods must be pursued in taking in and enclosing the commons. No further action was taken until 1795 when Mr. John Wade of Silsden was appointed to measure the commons at a fee of three guineas.

Nothing came of this and in 1803 Christopher Bradley was appointed to inspect the waste and prevent future encroachment. Later a mole catcher was appointed for an annual fee of ten guineas. By 1823 the town meeting agreed to let that part of the common to the north side of the projected new road from Addingham to Silsden, being part of Hunterlands. Ten years later it was proposed to appoint a herdsman as the manure and soil had been sold and taken away and cattle and sheep trespassed on the common.

Eventually, however, an Act for Enclosure was passed. Even then it took from 1866 to 1873 for the award to be authorised. About 730 acres were finally enclosed. The Commissioner said that the boundary between Silsden and Addingham was ill-defined and caused boundary stones to be erected from Shepherd's Hill to Draughton Moor. The main of the land was set out in allotments to the freeholders in proportion to the size of their holdings and was placed as near to their other land as could conveniently be. The rectory was given land in right of glebe and tithe. The Lord of the Manor got land in lieu of his rights to the soil. Public quarries were set aside for supplying stone and gravel for use on their freehold or leasehold sites. The surveyors of the highways were allotted one and a half acres to get stone to repair the roads. The Churchwardens and Overseers of the Poor were given four acres as a place for exercise and recreation of the inhabitants. Another four acres were given them as allotments for the labouring poor. The two fields owned by the charities each acquired a small enclosure which was sold to their benefit.

Some of the land was sold to defray the expenses of the enclosure – twenty-nine acres for £420. A few farms near the Low Moor were able to increase their land holdings with easily improvable land. The land on the Middle Moor was all reclaimed and much of the Low Moor has been improved also. Many of the smaller allotments were sold straight away and absorbed into larger areas. The prehistoric earthworks, barrows, Round Dykes and part of the circumvallation remain untouched.

The High Moor was divided into large allotments. The acid sandstone rock was very near the surface so that acid tolerating plants covered the ground as they still do. They are heather, bilberry, crowberry and poor grasses. On the steep escarpment bracken has taken hold. This used to be controlled as it was cut by scythe, burnt and the ash used as 'potass' (potash). This mixed with fat made a soap used for cleaning wool and cloth. Before enclosure cattle were turned out on the moor; they trampled the bracken and added a certain amount of manure to the soil.

Turning the Century

'It was evident' said the *Ilkley Gazette* in July 1875 'that Addingham which had been at a standstill for a long time was now awakening to the spirit of the age in the way of trade and building. Some years ago nearly one half of the houses stood empty but of late years all have become occupied and, now and again, a new house has been built and, as these have not been equal to meet the demand, rents have as a natural consequence been increased. ... building sites are not easily attainable ... the new day schools have been erected and a new weaving shed is very nearly completed which will require a considerable number of hands to keep its machinery in operation'. A building club had been formed which had acquired land opposite Mount Hermon chapel.

The reporting of events in the *Ilkley Gazette* shows that Addingham had a lively community. The mood of optimism resulted in Richard Smith of London, then Lord of the Manor, proposing to build twenty streets of houses, each between forty and fifty houses. He owned land in Aynholme and Capplegangs now occupied by sheltered housing and the Middle School. There were minor setbacks, Hartley and Hargreaves closed suddenly at Townhead Mill but it was soon re-opened after the former management (G.Prior) bought it.

Small shops still lined the Main Street. Grocers, greengrocers, butchers, drapers, ironmongers (Tinner Whitaker's), shoe shop, even a shoe factory for a short time, bakers and sweet shops provided most of the needs of the village. An Addingham Co-operative Society had started in Kitty Fold. It prospered sufficiently to buy land on Bolton Road and built new premises and a row of cottages. 'Pop' Harrison made lemonade in a building near the beck. He used the old fashioned bottles with a glass ball in the neck. The story is that he washed the bottles in the town beck as it passed his door. He also kept a druggist's shop. Doctors continued to live and practise in the village. It is said that Dr. Bates used to ride across the ford below the High Mill to visit his patients on the north side of the river. He took a servant, also on horseback, so that he could get his trap to send his patient to hospital if necessary. The old ferry which brought the Beamsley parishioners to church was superseded by a suspension footbridge and a horse bus connected with some of the trains at Ilkley.

The parish as a local government authority came to an end during the nineteenth century with reforms which created municipal and county boroughs and rural councils. Addingham became part of Skipton Rural District in the old West Riding, thus keeping its old and long connection with Craven. The Parish Council was established in 1894. Each parish council was required to have a parish meeting at least once a year. Although their powers are limited they are able to bring small, and sometimes not so small, local isssues forward. As successors of the old town meetings held by the independent inhabitants they carry on a tradition of three hundred years.

At the end of the century there were five textile mills working. Three of them, with the largest part of the workforce, were Listers'. Samuel Cunliffe-Lister had long left Farfield Hall for Swinton Castle at Masham. He had been created the first Baron Masham of Swinton and had stretched his business interests far and wide. He died in 1906 aged 91. His body, together with many mourners, was brought by special train from Masham to Addingham. He was interred in their vault in the church. The personal connection of the Cunliffes with Addingham had ended.

References

Rate Book. *WYJAS*. (Bradford).
Overseers of the Poor. *WYJAS*. (Bradford). 48D90.
Baines, 1822. *'Directory of the County of York'*.
Mrs. Gaskell, 1857. *'Life of Charlotte Bronte'*.
Rickard's Report.
Addingham Iris 1845-46. (Ilkley Library)
Cunliffe-Lister, Samuel., 1905. *'Lord Masham's Inventions'*. (Bradford).
Lemmon, W., *'The Story of an Addingham School'*. 1874 – 1974.
Charity Commission Report. I.F.P.I.G.
E.Lancs. Yorks. Railway Extension. Spencer-Clarkson Collection. (Keighley Local History Library)
Craven's Directory. 1884.

Chapter 7

The Making of Modern Addingham

The Railway at Last

THERE were a number of abortive attempts to bring the railway up the Wharfe valley. A proposal to bring the line up the north side of the Wharfe was blocked by the various influential landowners. In 1883 local promoters, together with the Midland Railway Company, put a Bill through Parliament for the Ilkley – Skipton extension. Many landowners must have thought that they would make money from selling their land to the railway company. One farm at least (Reynard Ing) was bought with that intention. In fact it balanced evenly between purchase and later sale.

The construction was carried out rapidly although it needed a number of bridges and viaducts. Two alternative routes were proposed to take it through Addingham. A low level route with the station practically on the Main Street with a level crossing across the main road or the higher level, with a bridge over, which fortunately was the one chosen. Navvies were brought in to work; many were Roman Catholic Irish, some of whom stayed in the village after the line was completed, forming a Roman Catholic community. The navvies were well paid and independent. One group working the Hollin Hall to Lumb Gill stint, perhaps the deepest cutting on the line, went on strike. They had been filling fifteen wagons in nine hours during the winter but, in summer, they were expected to fill seventeen wagons in ten hours. They were dismissed and new workers were employed.

For nearly two miles out of Ilkley the line closely followed that of the Roman road, made nearly two thousand years earlier, before the line swung away to Addingham station.

The opening of the railway between Ilkley and Addingham on Wednesday, May 16th, 1888 was an occasion for rejoicing celebrated in verse in the *Ilkley Gazette* by the Addingham poet, Thomas Whitaker;

> 'Hurrah for the Railway is opened at last,
> The bells are all pealing with joy;
> The village with beautiful banners is dress'd -
> Let nothing our gladness destroy.

The trains are gliding so softly along -
Like beautiful birds in their flight;
And ready to bear us away from the throng,
With engines all shiny and bright.

Then hurrah! for the engines now steaming along
And speeding so smoothly away;
And all the promoters and navvies so strong
Hurrah! hurrah! hurrah!'

The prospectus for the railway said that there might be as many as fifty trains a day from Skipton; far too optimistic an estimate and never likely to be achieved. After the line was open through to Skipton a train was run from Colne to Harrogate, making an easy crossing of the Pennines. One of the main advantages cited was that it would open lower Wharfedale to the inexhaustible limestone quarries of Skipton and Draughton. It is doubtful if the line ever made a profit and it did not live up to its rosy expectations. Lister's sent goods to and from their Manningham and Addingham mills for processing. Trees were brought for the sawmill. Coal, agricultural goods and groceries were carried – far below the anticipated carriage. A number of young men travelled from Addingham to Shipley to attend a course for 'Overlookers' at the Shipley Technical College. The train to return home only travelled as far as Guiseley and they walked the rest of the way. The line was very popular for excursions both to Bolton Abbey and beyond to Blackpool and Morecambe.

One of the consequences of travel by rail was the virtual abandonment of roads. As early as 1867 the *Ilkley Gazette* said that the bar hill to Addingham was almost impassable. The bulk of the limestone used on the Burley, Menston and Otley roads was carted from Draughton – about eighteen heavily laden carts almost daily during the winter season. The turnpike roads were losing revenue and were dispiked. The bars were abandoned and the gates were opened. Many of the Inns struggled to stay in business as the horse coaches were withdrawn. Road travel became mainly local; drovers and carriers still plied their trades and the poor people still walked. John England gave a good picture when he referred to the transfer of management of the roads from the old highway boards to Skipton Rural District Council in 1897. He said that 'Addingham roads had cost £620 a fearful amount of extravagance. The amount of stones laid on the roads had been something fearful. Hundreds of tons had been laid on from the Craven Heifer to Chelker when there was very little traffic and from the Craven Heifer to Cringles on which nothing but a few carts and conveyances travelled'. There was soon to be a revival on the roads. Six years after John England's remarks it was said that 'it was questionable whether any motorist existed who in a day's ride did not exceed the twelve miles an hour, provided the car was equal to it'.

The railway continued throughout both wars, bringing heavy chemicals along the line as well as passengers. We saw train loads of German prisoners but bus, coach and car were already competing. The two dreadful snowy winters of 1947 and 1962-3 showed the value of the rail track in this kind of weather when the roads over the Pennines were closed for about ten days and rail provided the only link to Skipton. The Ilkley-Skipton line was used to train the drivers of the new Diesels but it was to be swept away under the Beeching closures of 1965. The dismantling of the low bridges, the high embankment and the station followed quickly making land available for redevelopment.

Housing

Although the houses in Addingham were huddled closely together they were strung out over a mile on the sides of the Main Street. Traditional stone walls and stone slate roofs were used until it became easier to bring in red brick, Welsh slate and red roof tiles. The builders used local stone. There were many good local quarries. Vicar Wood earlier known as Spencer's Gill and now as Walker's Gill provided stone for building the church tower and continued in use until this century. Its stone built High House in the Main Street and Hallcroft. The last building in which it was used was the War Memorial.

There were two quarries at Crossbank. One was a public one set aside in the enclosure award; near it was a private quarry, both are now worked out. Stone from Crossbank is known to have been used in building houses in Turner Lane. Stone from the Brockabank Quarry built part of the 1925 mill at the Low Mill and was used, together with stone from Panorama Quarry in Ilkley, to build part of Peltzer's portion of the Low Mill. Other quarries were opened and used to repair the roads (Hunterlands, Paradise Delf and Stoop Quarry at Four Lane Ends). There were skilled masons such as the firm of Hargraves who built the Low Mill and made their weir. The Hargraves had a reputation as good and quick builders and once built a farmhouse in six weeks.

Buildings erected in the early nineteenth century often had an attractive type of tooled decoration on door jambs and window surrounds. Stone walls (particularly gables) were 'watershot', that is the stones were slightly set back in each course, the theory being that the rain would not penetrate between courses. Sometimes weather protection was given by rendering and whitewash which made a pleasing contrast to the grey stone. Unfortunately most of the stonework on these houses has recently been cleaned and repointed so that the contrast is lost.

During the nineteenth century houses were built as a speculation and for renting rather than for owner-occupation. There was no planning and probably building plots were bought in the hopes of making a good investment. The two-cell thatched cottages of which there is evidence in the Overseers accounts had long since disappeared. The 'Jolly Sailor' was recorded as a thatched house in the 1838 rate valuation but was replaced by the present stone building in that year. It is said that the last thatched cottage in Addingham was at or near Mount Hermon Chapel but it was never photographed.

Some of the stone built cottages which survived into this century were very small. They were nearly all condemned in the 1950's-60's and were demolished. Other cottages in Main Street, Cockshott Fold and Kitty Fold all disappeared. The sites which now remain as open spaces show how small these houses were. Nevertheless, in their turn, they had probably replaced much more damp and uncomfortable dwellings.

The workers' housing was added to in the later nineteenth century by back-to-back houses such as Victoria Terrace. Southfield Terrace is reputed to have been erected by a builder who was paid £87.10.0 for building each house out of which he had to pay the joiner and he had to complete one house each week.

Highfield House was built by lawyer Alcock of Skipton about 1780, one of the first of the more 'gentry' type of house. Here Mrs. Elizabeth Alcock looked after her dead daughter's children. The eldest, Henry Alcock Bramley, lived there quietly, his son, Henry Ramsden Bramley, was Dean of Lincoln Cathedral. Farfield House appears to be much the same period. Few larger houses were built until a speculative builder erected a short row at Springfield in the 1880's. There was now a demand for the large, solid, Victorian villa, lit by gas with gas lamps in the streets. There was the new sewage system and water from the Bradford supply and with a rail station in the village giving easy travel, living in such houses must have been comfortable and up-to-date.

Farfield Hall had been let by the Cunliffe-Lister family after they had vacated it to move to Swinton near Masham when Samuel Cunliffe-Lister was created Baron Masham of Swinton. After being rented to various tenants, Farfield Hall was sold to George Douglas, Chairman of the Bradford Dyers Association. He immediately started to remodel the garden and grounds reputedly employing 300 men to landscape the gardens and surroundings. He was careful to preserve the view of Beamsley Beacon and the heather moors to the north by keeping a gap in the trees and shrubs which were otherwise planted for privacy and shelter between the house and the road. George Douglas' son, Keith, became a musician and well-known conductor in London. His father converted a billiard room as music room as an extra wing to the Hall. This was elegantly furnished in the art deco style of the period (about 1929). On the death of Keith Douglas the Hall was offered for sale once more. At this time (1947) there was a great shortage of housing of all types. The West Riding County Council was seeking for buildings suitable for homes for old people needing care. They bought and converted the property which continued as an old folks' home until 1989 when it was sold into private ownership once more.

After World War I there was a need for smaller, cheaper, houses. Council houses were built up Moor Lane, probably on land owned by the Parish Council (sometimes known as Hospital Close). Private building also took place in Moor Lane. More Council houses were bult in School Lane, Burns Hill and Green Lane. After World War II sheltered housing was a priority. Small bungalows were built at Aynholme followed by single room dwellings at Southfield House and flats at Mount Pleasant. These replaced some of the very small older dwellings condemned and demolished by Skipton Rural District Council.

It was difficult to find land for new housing mainly because there was only limited access to possible building land behind the Main Street. Both sewage and water services were overloaded. These services were improved but access was more difficult. The Moor Park development made Long Addingham even longer. The demolishing of the station and the railway bridge over the Main Street allowed access to a considerable acreage of land at the Southfield for development. Bark Lane, which had been extremely narrow, was widened so that houses could be built on each side. A number of houses which narrowed the road in North Street were pulled down allowing more housing to be erected. At the same time the policy of condemning old properties ceased. It was recognized that many of these houses could be improved and renovated. Thus the two rows of back-to-back cottages in the Rookery, built about 1806, were converted into through houses and improvements were made in similar properties.

After World War II, in 1961, the West Riding County Council carried out a survey at Addingham considering its likely needs and development for the following ten years. They suggested that the slight fall in population was due to outward emigration in search of work. The survey showed that 55% of the working population worked in Addingham and another 23% worked in Ilkley. At this time the Sandbeds sewage treatment plant was grossly overloaded. Although one or two minor improvements were planned there was no intention of carrying out any major works – a decision soon to be reversed. The report stated that they did not expect any great growth before 1971 but made a proviso that there was an increasing mobility in the population which might lead Addingham to become a dormitory for larger towns. They foresaw a need to house or re-house about 450 persons (at 3 persons per household that would be 150 new houses). In fact it was not foreseen that the building of quite a large number of small, affordable, houses near Moor Lane would attract incomers who liked the area but found the houses in Ilkley too large, too inconvenient or too expensive to live in.

Services and Societies

In 1961 there was still a wide range of shops and most people did their shopping in the village. Grenville Holmes wrote a letter to the *Ilkley Gazette* in 1983 remembering that there were four butcher's shops, three grocers with corn merchants, two coal merchants and one each of:- blacksmith, cabinet maker, photographic studio, gents' outfitters, bespoke tailor, registrar, dentist, tinner's shop and mineral water manufacturer. 'We also had Conservative, Liberal, Cricket, Soccer, Rugby and Ladies' Hockey Clubs. Boy Scouts, Girl Guides, Cubs and Brownies, a Mechanics Institute, a Male Voice Choir, Parish Church, Wesleyan Chapel, Mount Hermon Chapel, Roman Catholic Church, several of which had good choirs and were well attended. The Church Sunday School was attended by over one hundred children in those days. We also had two missionaries one of whom was murdered in Johannesburg'. The list was by no means complete.

Electricity was first brought from Ilkley as late as 1928-9 when an 11,000 volt cable was laid to the Low Mill. This was extended to a sub-station behind Burnside Mill with a spur to Farfield Hall. The use of electricity spread only slowly to the cottages, many of the older people were suspicious of it and still used a candle to light them to bed.

The Mechanics Institute closed about 1930 and its interesting library was dispersed (it included Whitaker's *History of Craven* and Doughty's *Arabia Deserta*). A branch of the West Riding County Library was opened, at first for only four hours a week. The first librarian was Miss Woof, headmistress of the Church School. It was lifeline to many during long years of blackout and war. As soon as possible opening hours were expanded and both low rooms of the old school, which housed it, were utilised. There was a regular exchange of books by the excellent West Riding County Library. It is now part of the Bradford library service.

The Roman Catholic congregation, which had met in a room in William Lister's Tallow Chandlers premises, laid the foundation stone of their new church in 1927. In the 1930's an effort to buy the field by the Parish Church – the Church Orchard – was successful. It was bought by public subscription by many small efforts to raise the money and was presented to the church in 1935. The intention was to prevent it from being sold for building.

A small length of river bank, donated by John Dawson to the village, had always provided the possibility of free fishing and the length of bank was increased.

Clubs for special interest groups have formed, prospered and disappeared as need arose. Pigeons, Gardeners, Winemakers, Womens' Institute and others have superseded some of the earlier ones.

The shops in the village have changed much, due to the rise of the supermarket and much greater ease of travel. The grocers and sweet shops have suffered most. There was a period when there were four antique shops. Shops of character have disappeared. Sidney Steel's clog shop was a warm place to go and gossip, or 'cal' while a new clog iron was being put on. 'Tinner' Whitakers supplied old-fashioned hardware and once was able to find a piece of horn to repair an old horn lantern. He was also the village plumber. The Addingham Co-operative Society closed its doors about 1970 but made an ideal home for a potter and hand weaver.

When the Church School closed its foundation deed stipulated it had to be sold for the best price. It had served as a hall for the village for entertainments and meetings; fortunately the Memorial Hall became available and replaced it.

Farming

Farming practices altered little during the nineteenth and early twentieth centuries. The small farms of the seventeenth century looked practically the same two hundred years later. A stone farmhouse and a stone barn with housing for a horse, half a dozen cows, a few calves, perhaps a pig and a few hens. In the fields there were a few ploughed acres, perhaps an intake or a piece of enclosure improved in similar manner to Henry Harrison's 'Ruf Intake' (Chapter V). Grain could be bought more cheaply and easily than it could be grown in the damp and misty conditions of the Pennine hills. A small field of turnips, a few potatoes and perhaps an acre of oats was the limit.

Ilkley had grown to a sizeable town between 1870-1900. Moreover, the families who had come to live there required good quality food and living. Fresh milk and dairy produce from the Moorside farms supplied this demand. Chickens' eggs and fresh meat were all produced so that the farms remained viable after the handloom weavers had lost their trade.

The motive power was the horse aided by one or two primitive machines; a hay mower, horse driven, with reciprocating knives, had replaced the scythe; a hay tedder (turner), also horse drawn, helped along haytime – the most important crop. Milking was carried out by hand in mistals (cowsheds) lit by candlelight or primitive paraffin lamps.

Even at the outbreak of World War II the small farms kept the traditional ways. In one way wartime conditions and regulations perpetuated the old order. Much land had to be sown and cropped with cereals – mostly oats. The local farmers were ill-equipped both with power and machinery. The fickle climate made harvest chancy and difficult. There was a big demand for milk. Farms which had not produced milk for sale before were making milk – still by hand. There were probably only two farms in Addingham with milking machines and they had their own engine power. For some years after the war there was a continued shortage of food and there was a push to produce more and more from our own farms. By 1955 the country had recovered sufficiently to expand its electric grid and the Yorkshire Electric Power Company started an ambitious scheme to supply electricity to all the farms. The offer was taken up enthusiastically but few saw what changes it would bring in the future. Also after the war the development of the small Ferguson tractor, with hydraulic lift, (first petrol, then paraffin, then diesel powered) revolutionised work in the fields. The horse, as a source of power, had disappeared by 1960. The two new sources of power revolutionised farming forever. One person could milk sixty cows as easily as six. Similarly with field work – haymaking machinery and manure spreaders were developed specifically for tractors. As soon as was feasible the arable was laid to grass again. Agricultural policies encouraged milk production and, later, sheep. As it was possible to manage a far greater amount of livestock with the same amount of labour many of the small farms were no longer viable units. Farmers left to seek larger farms elsewhere or retired and sold or let their land to neighbours. As a result the number of working farms is now about a dozen, though the total acreage farmed is little less than it was a hundred years ago.

A small acreage of land, perhaps 150 acres, has been used for building and a certain amount of moorland edge land has been improved. In 1993-94 a nine hole golf course was made. Many of the traditional farmhouses have been sold and 'done up'. Others are lived in by retired farmers or those who have chosen other work. Few people, apart from farmers, would have lived in these farmhouses until the arrival of electricity and the motor car made living more comfortable and access more easy.

Improvements made to Moor Lane, which is used for access to the water works, opened the way to some farms. The lane to the farmhouses on the Moorside was an unadopted track fit only for horse drawn vehicles. The farmers combined and, with the help of a grant from the Ministry of Agriculture, brought the lane up to the standard that the highways department would maintain.

Probably the present trends will continue. Farm sizes may well rise further. A few farms will erect large sheds and the redundant farmhouses together with their stone barns will continue to be converted for private use. Many will wish to own a paddock to keep a horse or pony for recreation, thus creating quite a different type of recreational smallholding. More land may be taken out for leisure activities.

Textiles: Decline and Fall

Population – Twentieth century

1901	1911	1921	1931	1941	1951	1961	1971	1981	1991
2144	1987	1923	2005	not taken	1873	1763	2065	2600	2965

The population was fairly static during the first half of the century. The slight decline was perhaps due to smaller families and emigration of adult workers. People were also ageing and there was a larger than average number of old age pensioners. This ties in with the history of the mills. They too were old-fashioned and ageing. The mills never really recovered from the upheaval of World War I. One new weaving shed and factory was opened by Messrs. Adams using premises abandoned half-built by a bankrupt builder. First weaving cottons and artificial silks and later, knitting nylon fabric, it closed in 1958. Another small tape mill operated briefly and Lister's started to extend by building a new stone three-storeyed mill in 1925.

The textile trade was already depressed and the new mill was never fully occupied. Despite that fact Listers entered into a partnership with Peltzer Gebruder of Crefeldt in Germany in 1932. Duties on silk and velvet induced Peltzers to start weaving velvets in this country. Listers built new weaving sheds and Peltzers brought over advanced looms and some workmen. The yarn was spun and supplied by Lister. All went well until World War II when the velvet weaving shut down. Some of the German workmen were interned in the Isle of Man.

As with all other textile firms work was limited to the war effort. Lister's expertise with silk allowed them to produce 'shell cloth', parachute silk and cord, also camouflage cloth, battle dress cloths and utility cloth.

In 1941 the S.U. Carburettors factory in Coventry was bombed. Peltzers weaving shed was one of the sites to which production was moved and continued until 1945. The textile machinery was taken to Bradford and machine tools took their place. Up to 1000 people worked at S.U. Carburettors. Temporary houses ('prefabs') were erected in Ilkley for workpeople and many more were brought in by bus. An alternative electricity cable was brought over from Silsden in case the main supply from Ilkley was disrupted. Carburettor parts were made at Addingham and assembled elsewhere. After the war the manufacture of carburettors ceased and the work returned to Coventry. Textiles were in short supply and for a short time the mills were working hard but our buildings and machinery were old and as the continent rebuilt and re-equipped the British textiles manufacturers found themselves in difficulties. There was a major closure of cotton mills. Burnside, belonging to Listers, closed in 1948, followed by the

High Mill (also Listers) in 1953. Wolsey shed, which had been weaving artificial silks, closed the same year. Townhead continued until 1971. The spinning department at Low Mill ceased in 1967 and all other operations in 1976.

As the mills and textile buildings closed down some stood empty for a while; others were used for different purposes. The great weaver's shop became a shoemaking factory. The road outside was known as Cobblers Steps. Wolsey Shed and High Mill were occupied by light engineering firms. Burnside Mill, after being empty for many years, is now display space for stripped pine and other furniture. Townhead Mill houses a number of retail firms. The sawmill (originally Fentiman's cotton mill) was taken by W. Brear in the 1860's and used for many years as a chairmaking factory and general sawyer. This was powered originally from the dam, later by a gas engine and Pelton wheel, utilizing waste sawdust. Now its saws are powered by electricity. The chairmaking, which supplied local schools and meeting halls with seating, ceased, but sawing and planking continue.

Barcroft Shed, started by the Adams brothers, was sold to a firm manufacturing plastic sanitary ware. Known popularly as the 'plastics factory' the making of this type of product continued through a number of 'take-overs' – Bartol, Bathtubs, Cisterns, until it was finally acquired by Ramfield (Springram plc) who closed the works down. Since then permission has been given to change its use from industrial purposes to housing. Thus the last industry in Addingham has ceased.

Meanwhile, the two old mills at the Low Mill were demolished in the 1970's and the stone removed to build houses elsewhere. The workers' houses in the mill yard were refurbished and other new houses built. The later mill and weaving sheds have been used partly for storage and warehousing.

Charities

It will be remembered that the Charity Commissioners held an enquiry into the status of the Old School in 1892 which was resolved by creating the Old School Trust for educational purposes. There were another few small charities going back as far as 1685.

In 1685 John Dawson conveyed a small close by the river and the High Mill to the Overseers, the income from letting to be paid to the poor. Another field called Crossleys field or the Dole field was bought the same year when the Overseers had some money to invest. Widow Boocock and Parkinson each left £20, the interest on which was to be paid to poor people (widows in Boocock's case) who had no town's pay. This £40 was lent to the Church when it was being repaired in 1758. The Church paid interest until compulsory Church rates were abolished in the nineteenth century and the principal was lost. All these were noticed by the

Charity Commissioners. There was also another field called Stamp Hill which escaped their notice. No explanation has ever been found of how or when this piece of land came into possession of the township. It was here that the Overseers built a little house for the poor (the first 'Council house') and the piece of land still belongs to the village.

Other benefactions included about £100 left by John Cunliffe and more later by his widow Mary. This was invested in Consols by the Charity Commissioners. In the twentieth century various closes have been donated for recreational purposes. An Addingham inhabitant Mr. Hoffman Wood left a field between the Junction and New Road Top. This is used as a football field. He also left money, the income from which was to provide each school child with one shilling to start a savings account with the Yorkshire Penny Bank.

A farmer, Mr. A. Walker, left a field now called the amenity field. Part of this is now a football field and the lower portion is a very useful playground with swings and slides for small children.

During World War II a women's knitting circle was formed to provide comforts for the troops. At the same time they were aiming to raise money for a Memorial to the men and women of Addingham who had sacrificed so much for their homes and country. In 1946 they had £1,000 invested and a public meeting resolved that the memorial should take the form of a Village Hall.

For another 12 years an elected committee worked to raise more money. Horse races, Children's Days, Whist Drives and dances, and many more efforts raised the sum £3,790. The Primitive Methodist Chapel was vacant and was offered for £1000. This was ideal and the generous offer was accepted. Much more money was needed to pay for the conversion to a village hall.

Twenty years later a large legacy came to Ilkley and Addingham. James Clarke and his sister Sarah Foley had lived in Addingham and attended school there and in Ilkley until their parents took them to the U.S.A. When they died their considerable fortune was left to help and aid the older people of both Ilkley and Addingham. At this time there was a debt on the Memorial Hall which had been enlarged and improved. Money was contributed from the Clarke-Foley bequest to wipe out the debt and one of the rooms in the hall was named the Clarke-Foley room.

The central position of the Memorial Hall together with its car park, adjacent to the amenity field, the football field, the earlier War Memorial and bowling green make a very pleasant area in the village and make a natural south-easterly 'edge' to the built up area.

A large bequest was left also by James Clarke to the elderly of Addingham. At present this money is invested and the interest is distributed before Christmas to those who qualify (to have lived in Addingham two years and be on the electoral role) of pensionable age.

Before the war there was an Addingham Nursing Association supported by voluntary subscriptions who funded a District Nurse working in the area. She lived in a cottage down High Mill Lane. The Association provided her with a car and paid her a salary. From the accounts it seems that she paid about 250 visits a month and carried out a very valuable service to the villagers. After the formation of the National Health Service in 1948 the nursing association was wound up as the committee did not wish to work with the NHS and an Addingham Benevolent Trust was formed. In 1972 all the small charities were combined into the Addingham United Charities Trust for Relief in Need.

Education

At the beginning of the twentieth century there were two schools in Addingham. The 'High' Council School in premises built by the Wesleyans and the 'Low' School or Church School. The 'High' School had a new infants classroom to which the infants had been transferred from the Old School. High and Low refer to their relative positions in the village and had no other significance.

A report of 1905 gives the attendance figures as:-

	Numbers on register	Attendance	Halftimers
National mixed (Low)	121	108	10
Infants	53	44	
Wesleyan mixed	172	144	16
Infants	76	52	

No secondary education was available in the village and the school leaving age had not yet been raised to fourteen. The few children who continued at secondary school had to travel to Skipton, Keighley or Ilkley.

There was great stability in the schools during the first half of the century. Little change took place at the 'High' School and most of the staff served for many years. Mr. Harry Hewerdine was appointed head in 1885 and retired in 1923. He worked in the old system with enormous classes and the aid of monitors as teachers. Nevertheless he was able to teach a deaf and dumb boy to read and write. He was followed by Mr. W. Lemmon (1923-1952) who took the school through World War II with all the problems relating to it. He inaugurated a school meals scheme and instigated the building of a youth hut next to the school kitchen which served a dual purpose as school dining room and a meeting hall. Mr. Lemmon was very interested in, and carried out research on, local history which he made the linchpin of his teaching of history and geography. Other staff included Mrs. Milford, 'Miss Emily' Cockshott and Miss Edith Cockroft, all remembered with affection and gratitude by the infants who came into their care not so much for their teaching but because the little children, who all walked to school, sometimes arrived very wet indeed. They were all dried and warmed and their clothes were also dried on the central heating pipes.

Mr. Sidney Simpson replaced Mr. Lemmon in 1952. Already the Education Act of 1944 had made changes. The 11+ examination (Thorne scheme) had started a selection system. Those who passed could go to a Grammar School – boys to Ermysted's School, Skipton or to Ilkley Grammar School, girls to Skipton High School for Girls. The remainder were sent on to a secondary modern school in Silsden. The parent-teachers group was founded and swimming instruction introduced, at first at the Ilkley Grammar School, then at the Ilkley indoor pool. The present head, Mrs. J. Jones, has been awarded the MBE for her innovative teaching. The 'Low' school had been losing scholars as the houses on the way to the Low Mill became empty and the population tended to go to the higher end of the village. Miss Elsworth, their head of some years, handed her children over to the top school in 1961 and the two schools were amalgamated.

From the beginning of the century inspectors' reports had emphasised the inadequacies of the school buildings. A number of efforts were made to improve or replace the old buildings although none had succeeded. The Wesleyans, however, had other plans. They had decided to sell their old place of worship and to convert the school into a new chapel. They gave notice to the West Riding education authorities of their intention which resulted in the building of two classrooms, a hall and kitchen on a new and very pleasant site nearby. Mobile classrooms were added followed by an extension in 1976 (by this time it was part of the Bradford school system).

In the meantime the West Riding had re-organized its education system into three tiers. The 11+ (eleven plus) selection was discarded. First schools took pupils until they were nine when they moved to Middle schools and, at fourteen to Senior schools. The children who had been attending Silsden school were moved to Ilkley Middle School and on to Ilkley Grammar School. The Ilkley Middle School was expanding and a search for a site for a Middle School at the west side of Ilkley was fruitless. Eventually a good site was found in Addingham on the field called Capplegangs near to the First School and with plenty of land for playing fields and recreation.

There were no school governors in early days, a group of managers looked after the fabric of the buildings and appointed the staff, particularly the head teachers. The connection was severed when the new school was built. Although there is no formal provision, the Wesleyan Minister for the time being has always been appointed a governor. The schools have had many changes in the last twenty years, with changes in administration and curriculum. It is hoped that they will be able to settle down, for we are proud of our schools in Addingham, in the dedication of the staff and the success of their pupils.

Transport and the Bypass

The A59 and A65 are major routes across the Pennines and both affect Addingham closely. They have connected important centres in Yorkshire and Lancashire for many centuries. In early years Wakefield needed a route to Lancaster. Knaresborough also had links with Lancaster. Wakefield and the South needed a route up the west towards Kendal and Carlisle. All these made use of the Aire Gap. In the nineteenth century routes between the textile districts of the West Riding and Lancashire were necessary. The turnpike roads running along the narrow parallel valleys of the Aire and Wharfe provided the way.

We have seen how the Otley-Skipton and Otley-Colne-Blackburn turnpikes gradually evolved and improved as need arose. After the invention of the motor vehicle the road gradually replaced the railway in importance. The bus became the common form of conveyance, particularly during the period of petrol rationing in and after World War II. It was realised early in the century that Addingham had a winding, narrow and dangerous Main Street and in 1927 surveyors laid out a bypass line to the north of the village. Construction was delayed because of the depression of the 1930's. Ten years later moves had begun towards its construction. Negotiations to acquire the necessary land had started and the line was marked out when World War II brought all such work to an end.

In 1961 work started on the part of the new road to the east of Addingham. This piece of pre-war planning had been authorised and the money set aside for it. The road was moved away from the river bank, where Thomas and Rosamund Wade had had such trouble in the seventeenth century. (This continues today, a few years ago part of this road subsided nearly into the river.) A new three lane highway (now reduced to two lane) was made to Addingham where it joined the New Road Top (the *New Road* of the 1830's). The rest of the 1927 line was abandoned as inadequate and houses were gradually built on most of the land so released.

A proposal was made to widen the narrow, winding Back Beck Lane which resulted in a public enquiry. The total mood of the village was against. It was realized that it would become a mini-bypass and would delay other improvements. The narrow parts of North Street were widened by demolishing old cottages and Bark Lane, also very narrow, was widened; houses now line each side.

Pressure continued for a new bypass but only in 1989 did this come to fruition. The line taken by the new bypass (a two lane road with slow lane up the hill) is to the south of the village. Interestingly enough it cuts diagonally across the Roman Road made two thousand years ago. The new roundabout serves Silsden, the Aire Valley and Lancashire. But there are still problems with traffic wishing to travel from the Aire Valley to Wharfedale and the north-east which tries to find a winding way through the village.

There is no doubt that Addingham has both lost and gained through these changes to the roads. The widening of the country lanes has meant a loss of character of the countryside. On the other hand there are still many pleasant footpaths and narrow lanes. Care has been taken to plant trees and many bulbs on the verges, but do they compensate for the varieties of wild flowers and butterflies which have been displaced? The aspens and bird cherries in the wood at Cocken End were cut down to make way for our three lane road. The moisture loving and lime loving flowers in the same wood and on the sides of the railway cuttings have gone, together with the dragonflies on the river.

There are problems still looming. Bank holidays make congestion with pleasure traffic up Wharfedale briefly choking the roads in their journey home. A more permanent feature will be the proposed Ilkley bypass which seems likely to be an intrusive feature as it crosses the river on a bridge or raised way and then will make a great gash through the hills.

Planning and Conservation

The re-organisation of local government just before the twentieth century (1894) meant a big change in the administration of services for the village. Skipton Rural District Council was created to administer local services under the overall control of the West Riding County Council. The 'select vestry' disappeared to be replaced by the elected Parish Council. A rural district councillor also represented the village. The Parish Council had, and still has, only limited powers but it can act as a pressure group. It represents village opinion and its relationship to the earlier 'vestry' and town meetings can be clearly seen.

It was fortunate that the tradition of building in stone lasted until building in the centre of the village was complete. The stone buildings from the seventeenth to the twentieth centuries have given a unity to the Main Street which is now recognized in the conservation area. Brick and red tile, so out of place in the area, were barely used. There were, however, worrying trends. Insensitive alterations and unsympathetic new materials led to planning controls.

No-one knew how many old buildings there were until the organization, by

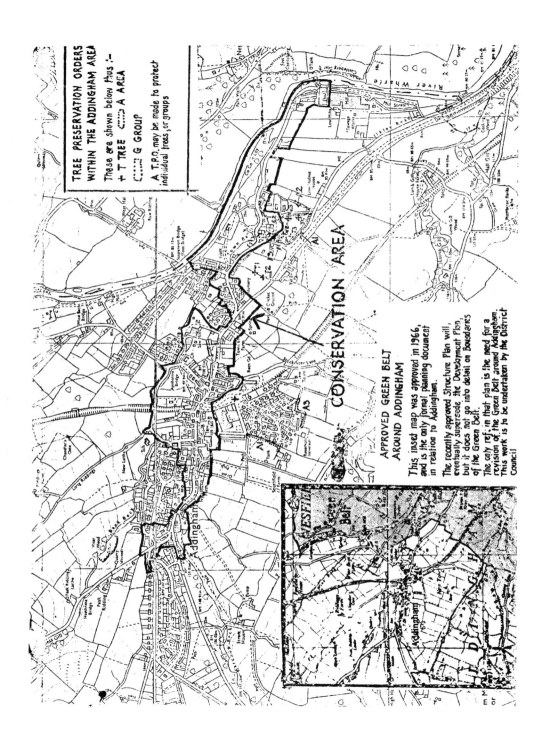

TREE PRESERVATION ORDERS
WITHIN THE ADDINGHAM AREA

These are shown below thus :-

+ T TREE ⟨⟨⟨⟩ A AREA

⟨⟨⟨⟩ G GROUP

A T.P.O. may be made to protect
individual trees, or groups

CONSERVATION AREA

APPROVED GREEN BELT
AROUND ADDINGHAM

This inset map was approved in 1966,
and is the only formal planning document
in relation to Addingham.

The recently approved Structure Plan will
eventually supersede the Development Plan,
but it does not go into detail on Boundaries
of the Green Belt.

The only ref: in that plan is the need for a
revision of the Green Belt around Addingham.
This work is to be undertaken by the District
Council.

the Department of the Environment which 'listed' into three categories the houses of architectural or historic interest. Fifty houses were placed on this first list including, as Grade I, the Church of St. Peter and Farfield Hall together with the Farfield Quaker Chapel which was given Grade II*. A resurvey of listed buildings was made in 1985. As a result another 69 buildings and other objects were added to the earlier list. These included boundary stones and guide stones, bridges, barns and a number of scattered seventeenth and eighteenth century farmhouses which had not been included in the first list. Ancient monuments scheduled include Round Dikes and the Church Orchard.

Since that time the need for some planning and control has increasingly been recognized. The survey of 1961 carried out by the West Riding County Council has already been mentioned. It was not long before attitudes changed. The demolishing of the railway station together with its bridge over the road and embankment allowed a new access onto the Main Street and opened up quite a large area. The water supply and sewage systems, which were overloaded, were improved allowing more houses to be built. Planning at this time was carried out by the Skipton Rural District Council whose policy was to condemn what was considered sub-standard housing. In 1973-4 local government re-organization placed Addingham together with Ilkley in the Bradford Metropolitan District under the new West Yorkshire County Council. Instead of being in the centre of the large administrative district of the old West Riding we found the village on the border with North Yorkshire. This disrupted the old connections, particularly patterns of schooling. All the services, from schools and roads to responsibility for grass cutting and flower beds, were transferred to Bradford. This brought us into different planning departments, for the first time to look towards Keighley and Bradford rather than towards Skipton.

The green belt policy was developed first in the 1960's as an attempt to protect land near the cities. Conservation areas were drawn up to protect the older or core areas of towns and villages.

The conservation area for Addingham was drawn in 1966 together with some tree preservation orders. It takes in land and buildings from the Green and Townhead down the Main Street and many of the buildings in the little side streets down to Church Street and Town End. The Church and its environs and Low Mill Lane as far as the old mill houses are included (see map).

The green belt incorporated open country to the south and east of Addingham as far as the border with North Yorkshire at the river Wharfe. North of the village the open country is designated as a special landscape area which, we are assured, is considered a more appropriate protection than the green belt. The green belt in Wharfedale was revised in the mid-1980's when small portions next to the village were removed from the map.

An Addingham village plan was drawn up in November 1986. Subject to an enquiry, the objective was to prepare a framework for development control decisions within the village. 'The fundamental issue has been the village's ability to accommodate future growth in a way that is sensitive to its attractive landscape setting'. The enquiry was to determine the policy towards various small green fields and crofts in the village. Each was examined individually and recommendations made about future function.

The report at that time said Addingham was not a growth point for future housing development either in relation to Wharfedale or the Metropolitan area as a whole. An enquiry into the boundaries between districts and counties in 1989 gave an opportunity to redraw the boundary between North Yorkshire and the Bradford Metropolitan District to follow the mid-line of the river, thus doing away with the anomalies of small pieces of land on the south bank, such as Wade Holm, which had gone into North Yorkshire.

A mandatory enquiry started in 1993 into the Unitary Development Plan. This was part of a nationwide enquiry. Bradford was instructed to find and reserve areas for housing and employment extra to those already set aside. The future depends very much on the planners. Industry has disappeared from the village and seems unlikely to return. Apart from local tradesmen and self-employed people everyone has to travel out of the village to work. We have seen how Addingham has slowly changed through the centuries from a small village obtaining most of its necessities within its own boundaries, through the textile era of the eighteenth and nineteenth centuries, where almost all of the inhabitants (male and female) worked in textiles. Now all industry has gone, we are a commuter village. This is partly due to our position with good natural routeways which connect us with other centres of industry, but also to our place as one of the 'Gateways to the Dales'.

We cannot foresee the future, but modern industry has passed us by. Perhaps the answer will come with the communications revolution, but more likely in ways that we cannot yet see.

Chapter 8

A Walk around the Boundaries

The Bounder of Addingham, 1608, rediscovered 1723

COPY of the Bounder of Addingham as it was delivered in by Mr. Wullm Vavisor then Lord of the Manor, the 23 May 1608, the Originall whereof I found among my Lords papers in the Evidence Room at Skipton Castle, which when I shew'd Mr Mires after I had Ridd the Bounders of Silsden in the sumer 1723 he did acknowledge and was satisfyed that my Lds Bounders were Ridd right, Mr Mires is now Lord of the Manor of Addingham. Chris Petyt.

> *The Bounder of Addingham*
> Beginning at the East part thereof, at the East Yeate or Cocken End, then to the River of Wharfe, then up the River till Lockwood (sic) Beck run into Wharfe, then to Slapestone Yeate, then to Lockwood (for Lobwood) Hedge, following the Hedge till you come to Chelkar head, then to Barwick Cawsey, then to Whitewell, then to Vavasor Chair, then to Thief Thorn, then to Knottendstone, then on Skipton Yate to a Cawsey wear Baxton Barr made and repaired amicably by the Inhabitants of Addingham, then to the west side of Semer Tarne, then to West Winyate Nick then to Threnopike, then directly North to East Yeate where wee began.
>
> (from a document held by the YAS)

Boundaries of the Manor of Addingham, c.1750

Beginning at Newstoop at the corner of Wade Holme, and so up the Inclosed Lands as the Parish of Addingham divides from Ilkley to the common, and so up the common directly south to the end of a Hill on the East side of a place called Shepherd House, and from thence turns westward, a good space south of the great Cart Gate, and so by several stones to a place called Double Stones (an Ancient Landmark) from thence to the west side of the Little Nick, being betwixt the Little Nick and the Cragg End, and so down the hill to an Intack wall, where

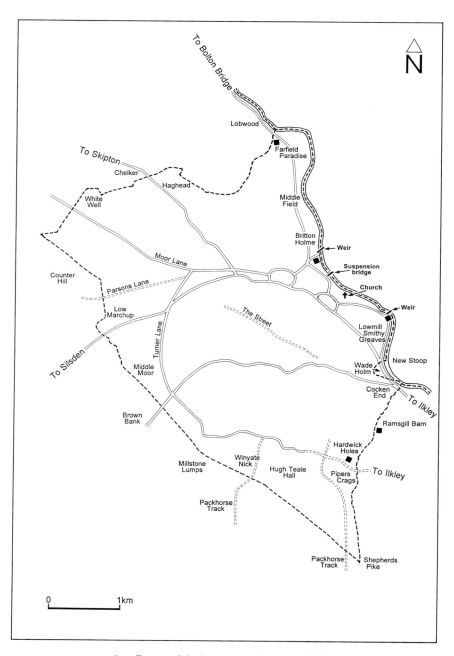

0   1km

A walk around the boundaries. *Drawn by WYAS.*

a bush stood into an intack called Brownbank Intack, and so Northwest to some Inclosures on the south west side of Seamer Tarn, and down those Inclosures into a Road that leads to Megarileys, and so following the way up Wolfa Bank, and down the way at the North end of the said Bank and so crossing the roads, goes up Jennings Intacks, directly to a place called Thief Thorn and from thence directly Eastwards along the south side of a great hill to a stone called Vavasor Chair, and so on by the White Well to the upper end of Chelcar, and so following the fence down the south side of Chelcar to Hagg Head, and so on the south side of Lob Wood and betwixt Lob Wood and Farfield Lands, by an Ancient Fence, down to the River Wharfe and so down the midstream where the Boundaries began.

(by Richard Smith, Lord of the Manor, quoted in the *Bradford Antiquary*, 1940, p. 402. Note that part of Beamsley was also in the parish of Addingham. This consisted of three or four farms inextricably linked with the other part of Beamsley, which was in Skipton.)

A Walk around the Boundaries

The boundaries of the ancient townships are often themselves very old. They enclose, in most cases, the variety of ground necessary for the sustenance of the village. Water, shelter, arable, meadow, pasture, woodland, moor and waste are all included. 'Waste' itself contained many important resources. Many parts of the boundary may have been determined before or soon after the Norman Conquest.

The boundary was usually seen as very important and encroachment by a neighbour was resisted. Some boundary accounts were written down very early and it was customary, as the phrase goes, to 'perambulate' them. The village officers together with the parson and the Lord of the Manor would walk around the boundary, usually on Holy Thursday, in every third year. The churchwardens' accounts for Addingham record spending 14s. on a perambulation in 1690. It is still legal for village officials to 'beat the bounds'. It is not always easy as there is rarely a footpath to follow and there is no obligation to provide stiles or crossing places. There are a number of boundary accounts for Addingham.

The account of 1750 begins, as it says, at the 'New Stoop' (a stoop is an elongated stone or wooden post). This is built into the wall near the river (SE09024880). This stone, which has a benchmark on it, marked the boundary between Nesfield and Addingham. At this point Nesfield came south of the river and enclosed a field called Wade Holme and part of the Sandbeds. The boundary proceeds clockwise eastwards along the river Wharfe beside the old road to Ilkley, along the river bank so carefully repaired and maintained by Thomas and

Roasamund Wade (Chapter III). The road is now part of the 'Dalesway' (a footpath from Ilkley to Windermere).

Ramsgill Beck enters the river from the south at Cocken End. Here, in the middle of the river, the three wapentakes of Staincliffe, Claro and Skyrack meet. An old ford crossed the river, a continuation of a packhorse track which wended northward over the moors. The boundary follows Ramsgill Beck southward as it defines the township, wapentake and parliamentary boundaries and was also the old boundary of Craven. The Roman Road also crossed Ramsgill, probably just above the waterfall where hard Millstone Grit rocks overlie the shales. Eighteen hundred years later the railway chose practically the same crossing.

In 1598 the Ilkley Court Rolls recorded that John Holmes took the waste near Ramsgill Beck at 2s. yearly. He made a good farm out of this land, a long strip on each side of the beck which extended from the Wharfe to the unenclosed moor. He built his farmhouse near to the beck at Netherwood. This has disappeared though the barn remains. Here too an old footpath from Addingham to the west end of Ilkley crossed the boundary. This footpath was much used by workmen living in Addingham and working as builders or quarrymen in Ilkley but it has been disused for many years.

As the boundary ascends towards the moor the land gets steeper and rougher. It passes Hardwick Holes, a small farm where a family of woolcombers lived. Here too was another track proceeding towards Ilkley. If it had not been for the intransigence of the then owner of Hardwick Holes, who refused to sell any of his land, a through road would have been made from Silsden to Ilkley. Upwards still to the moor plateau at Piper's Crag (miswritten Viper's Crag in the tithe apportionment).

Thence along the level moor the ground is thin and peaty with acid soil and covered with heather or, in wetter places, with cotton grass and bog plants. Once on the moor the boundary is less defined. There are boundary stones marked M (Middleton), G (Greenwood of Netherwood) and ILB (Ilkley Local Board). These go as far as the wall at Shepherd's Hill – formerly called Ralph's Pike or Threnopike. The old packhorse track going south-north from Airedale to Cocken End crosses the boundary just to the west of Shepherd's Hill.

From Shepherd's Hill to Draughton Moor the boundary was shared with Silsden. The whole length was in dispute during the seventeenth and eighteenth centuries; it was not determined until the enclosure of Silsden Moor. It passes Hugh Teal Hall (Hall meaning corner). Hugh Teal lived at Gill House in 1620. Another ancient track comes up the steep moor passing old quarry dressing floors through the Winyate Nick (the Little Nick) towards the Aire valley. This track gave access to old coal pits on Holden Moor where bell pits of early mining are thickly scattered. Later the same track may have been used as a drove road for the Scottish cattle which were driven from the summer pastures at Malham to the markets of South Yorkshire and the Midlands.

From Hugh Teal Hall a wall was built after the Addingham Moor enclosure of 1875. The line was first marked out at the Silsden enclosure act of 1773-5 but it was only marked with a few boundary stones. The Silsden enclosures took most of the old millstone quarry (Chapter V), so long in dispute with Addingham. Many of the millstones were transported up a worn and deep track (Winyate or Windygate Nick proper) onto the moor for transport to Otley and the east.

Having entered the pastures once more the boundary crosses the old road to Silsden (known as Brown Bank), then an open unwalled track, at a place marked by a boundary stone which probably replaced an old stone called Wildman Stone. Further on comes Seamer Tarn to the south on the Silsden side of the boundary. The tarn was drained in the seventeenth century when the men of Silsden asked permission to make a drainage ditch through Addingham lands. This is Addingham Middle Moor through which the Barden aqueduct and Nidd water pipe are brought on their way to Bradford. The 'new' Silsden road is crossed at Middle Marchup around the lands of Low Marchup farm – a farm probably made out of the Town Intack.

Next comes Parson's Lane which is mentioned in the Addingham enclosure award but is probably much older. It is a paved track, perhaps another drove road which becomes lost in the network of lanes on Silsden moor. Much of this boundary was under hot dispute. It was awarded to the Vicar of Kildwick in the Silsden enclosure award. This was the area where the Addingham freeholders pulled down the new enclosure fences.

The old accounts say that the boundaries met at Thief Thorn, a place marked on the O.S. map of 1845, but it is not on the later boundary. Neither is the next stone known as Vavasour Chair and we must assume that both were lost to Silsden. (Thief Thorn is said to be an Anglo-Saxon name for a gooseberry bush.) The boundary turns east against Draughton Moor and is crossed by the old coach road to Skipton as it runs through Addingham Low Moor, skirting White Well farm to Hag Head, the *Haia* of Alice de Romilly's charter of 1155, 'and betwixt Lob Wood and Farfield lands, by an Ancient Fence, down to the River Wharfe'. The 'ancient fence' was described as the *fossato de bailiwick* in two of the oldest deeds – that is the ditch of the township. The ancient fence has long gone to be replaced by a modern wall which still follows the same line.

'And so down the midstream where the boundaries began'. This laconic phrase does not describe the river banks or their appurtenances. The little boundary stream is now a mere trickle, perhaps when it was first made a boundary mark it carried more water and made a more obvious division between Draughton and Addingham. The footpath along the river bank, now part of the Dalesway, starts its way through 'Paradise', a field which already had that name in 1660. Then come Middle Field and Longlands, part of the arable land, to Britton Holme, owned by Adam de Brereton in the thirteenth century. The corn mill with its later textile mill extension drew water from the river using a very ancient weir which crossed the river in a long diagonal. Next to the mill is the small field given by John Dawson in 1685, the income from which was to be for the use of the poor. Children of the village have spent many hours playing in the river which is very shallow here. The shallow river was fordable and was used by travellers to Nesfield and Beamsley. It is remembered that Dr. Bates used this ford to visit his patients north of the river.

A ferry made a crossing at the head of North Street (formerly called Scar Top) until it was replaced by a foot suspension bridge (1890). It was near the ferry that J.M.W. Turner sat to paint his watercolour of the High Mill with the hills of Wharfedale in the background. The churchgoers of Beamsley, part of which was in the parish of Addingham, used this. In the next field, known as the Church Orchard, stands the Church and here too stood the former Hall or Manor House which fell into the river Wharfe. At the east end the town beck discharges into the river followed again by common arable fields known as Hallcrofts, Short, Middle and Long Holmes until the river turns abruptly at Nesfield Scar making a field known as Smithy Greaves. This field, extraordinarily, has had three industrial uses. The first explains its name, for 'Greaves' means a quarry and iron ore from the cliffs of Nesfield Scar was washed across the river to be dug out for smelting at Plumtreebanks. In the river, washed down from its headwaters, are piles of limestone pebbles. These were carted out of the river and burnt in various kilns along the river banks. Thomas Robinson of Nesfield made his will in 1722 leaving to his son Thomas liberty 'to get and gather limestones in the said Sandbeds and Smithy Greaves and burn the same in the limekiln there'. The third industrial use was of John Cunliffe's worsted spinning mill.

So we return along the river by the old mill goit, now sadly neglected and derelict, to the New Stoop, which seems to have disappeared in recent repairs, where the account began.

References

DD 121/79. Yorkshire Archaeological Society.
The Boundaries of the Manor of Addingham, *BA*, Volume 8, 1940, p. 403.

Appendix

An Archaeological Survey at Plumtree Banks, Addingham

Stephen Moorhouse

AN extensive multi-period earthwork complex lies between the Hall Gill and Lumb Gill, centred on Plumtree Banks Barn. The original intention was to record the earthworks of the late mediaeval iron working complex on the Hall Gill immediately east of Plumtree Banks Barn but it soon became clear that in order to understand the industrial complex the multi-period landscape between the two gills had to be surveyed. A total of 23 intermittent days was spent recording in January and February 1992 using triangulation based on a 50 metre grid oriented on the cardinal points.

Earthwork description

The area surveyed was bounded by Cocking Lane and Lumb Gill Lane on the north, a north-south line just east of Gate Croft Farm on the west, an east-west line south of the farm on the south and a north-south line east of Reynard Ing on the east. The earliest landscape features appear to be the remnants of a terraced rectilinear field system overlain by ridge and furrow ploughing of various widths. This is particularly distinct in the area to the west and south of the Hall Gill and of the barn. That between the Hall Gill and Reynard Ing is narrow and straight and suggests a recent origin. That to the west of the footpath from Cocking Lane to Gate Croft Farm is broader and of varying widths. That adjacent to the western side of the track is straight while that further west is broader and reverse 'S' shaped in plan, suggesting it is the oldest ploughing to survive, and may be mediaeval in date. It is this block to the west of the track that overlies an earlier landscape, comprising terraced field areas and probable building platforms. Their precise form is uncertain because of the subsequent ploughing. A series of buildings (a,b) appear to be contemporary with the earliest reversed 'S' ploughing. The absence of shallow banks as outlines for the structures suggests that they were of timber and their long narrow plans suggest a pre-16th century date, as suggested by work elsewhere in the Yorkshire Dales.

Four areas not associated with ridge and furrow deserve comment. An area on

Fig. 1
Plumtree Banks. Earthwork complex between the Lumb Gill and the Hall Gill. Letters refer to discu

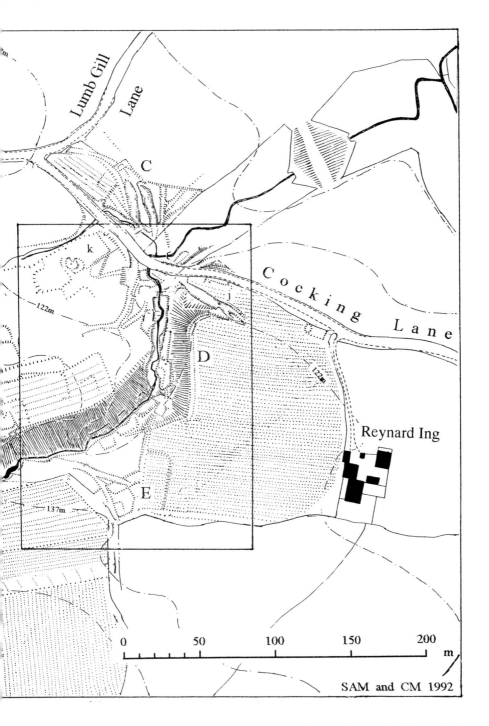

Lumb Gill
Lane

C

Cocking Lane

k

122m

j

D

122m

Reynard Ing

E

137m

0   50   100   150   200
m

SAM and CM 1992

the text, capitals to earthwork groups and lower case to earthwork features. For details of the enclosed
ame see Fig. 2.

the hillside in the angle of the Lumb Gill and Cocking Lane (A) contains a series of large terraced areas for rectangular buildings set within enclosures. The surviving broad reverse 'S' shaped ridge and furrow respects these earthworks, suggesting that they are contemporary, and therefore of probable mediaeval date. The absence of banks on the building platforms suggests that the structures were of timber. The more southerly ones are substantial and suggest barns. Access to the earthwork complex is by a field route (c) which turns northwards down the slope to Cocking Lane.

The second and more impressive earthwork complex lies around Plumtree Banks Barn (B). That to the east (d) is represented by a series of rectangular depressions on the flattened top of an eminence above the Hall Gill. To the north lie a series of parallel terraces on the hill slope (e). These have been truncated on the north by the canalisation of a spring which now flows into the Hall Gill to the north of the present bridge crossing. To the south and west of the barn lie a series of rectangular terraces and earthwork buildings (f), set around and within a large natural depression to the north of the Hall Gill. The track between Cocking Lane and Gate Croft Farm defines the north-western limit of these buildings. The stretch of this track towards the Hall Gill (g) appears to have been wider as it now lies in the centre of a much wider hollowed track, which had a series of rectangular timber buildings on its southern side (h). Immediately west of the barn the track overlies the platforms of at least five timber buildings (i), which are clearly earlier than the present track line and suggests that access was by another route. Earthwork terraces and banks run north-westward from the pre-track buildings but are destroyed by the ridge and furrow ploughing and they had clearly been abandoned before the track and ploughing to the west came into use.

The third complex (C) lies between the intersection of Cocking Lane and Lumb Gill Lane. It comprises successive earlier hollow way routes which predate the line of Cocking Lane to the east of its intersection with the top of Lumb Gill Lane. These curve round in a southerly direction, their outlet going westward up the slope to the complex on the hill top (B) above the Hall Gill. At least three successive hollow ways can be identified, up to 3 metres deep. A further well defined hollow way (j) lies to the south of Cocking Lane on the eastern bank of the Hall Gill. This appears to be an earlier line of the present road east of the bridge, and a natural extension of the line of Cocking Lane from its junction with Lumb Gill Lane and the bridge. It only survives for a short distance, where it climbs the valley side of the Hall Gill, and has been ploughed out when it reaches flatter ground. A series of terraced enclosures and possible buildings lie immediately to the west of Cocking Lane (k). They are truncated on the north by the modern canalized course of a spring which runs into the Hall Gill north of

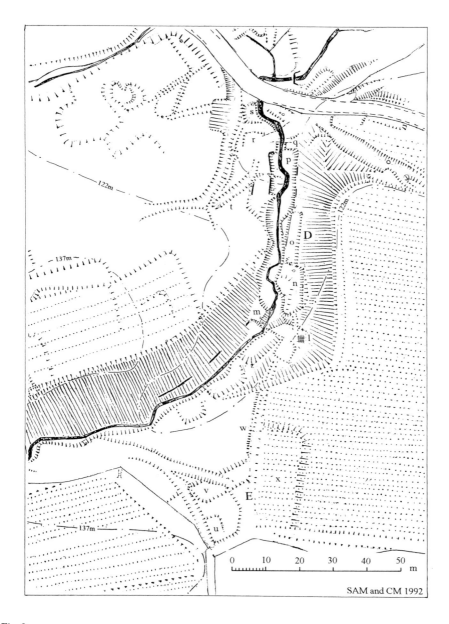

Fig. 2
Plumtree Banks. Earthworks of late mediaeval iron working complex on the Hall Gill. The setting is given in Fig. 1. The letters refer to descriptions in the text.

the bridge and on the east by Cocking Lane. They appear to have had modern disturbance on them.

The fourth group (D) was the initial purpose of the field survey (Fig. 2). It lies in the steep-sided valley of the Hall Gill, south of the bridge which carries Cocking Lane across it. The presence of an iron working site here was recognised many years ago by Mrs. Kate Mason, who found iron slag in a small mound on the southern bank of the gill (l). Further investigation by Mrs. Mason and the writer revealed an extensive and substantially complete water-powered iron smelting and forging site, which provided the impetus for the present survey. The grass covered slag heap lies immediately west of a substantial but now breached dam (m) which spans the Hall Gill. Boulder revetting is evident on the southern side, which continues along the steep northern slope of the Hall Gill for about 70 metres, shown in solid black line (Fig. 2). Vestiges of further boulder wall revetting lies further upstream to the west (Fig. 1). Adjacent to the dam (n), northwards on the eastern side of the gill, lies a rectangular terraced area, which is cut into the hillside on the east, with signs of revetting coming through the turf, and terraced up into a level platform on the west, where there is heavy boulder revetting between the platform and the gill. The walling here has been partially washed away over the years. A further long narrow terraced area (o) lies north of this platform, similarly partially revetted where it is cut into the hillside on the east and by heavy boulder stones on the gill side. Between here and the bridge lie the disturbed remains of a rectangular pond (p), with a dam at its northern end (q). The pond is revetted on its east and west sides with boulder stones and on the southern side of the dam. A terraced area (r) cut into the hillside on the west and terraced up on the north lies immediately west of the dam, with a further square terraced area (s) immediately north on the western side of the gill. A well-defined trackway (t) comes diagonally down the slope but stops short of the eastern side of pond p. It is truncated on its western side by the latest of the series of hollow ways which underlie Cocking Lane and give access to the structures represented by earthwork complex B. This single association shows that the iron working complex in the valley of the Hall Gill is earlier than the complex on the hill top above.

A further group of earthworks lie on the southern side of the Hall Gill valley (E), defined by modern field walls on the west and south. They contain a series of terraced enclosures, with at least two building terraces. The more southerly (u) is the more pronounced and stonework protruding through the grass suggests it may have been of stone. The more northerly (v) is badly truncated by a modern trackway climbing the hill slope. Although clearly terraced into the hillside there is no trace of stone and it was probably of timber. The eastern part of the complex is covered with straight narrow ridge and furrow ploughing which terminates on the eastern side of a terraced way (w) which leads from the earthwork complex to the iron working site in the valley below. The ridge and furrow has ploughed over a large raised enclosure (x) adjacent to the eastern side of the terrace way.

Interpretation

Earthwork Group A (Fig. 1)

The group of earthworks appears to represent a series of enclosures with timber buildings on terraced platforms. The larger and more southerly platforms suggest large barns, while those on the hill slope are small and, by the relationship of the platforms, successive buildings. The relationship of the earthwork group to the broad reverse 'S' shaped ridge and furrow ploughing suggests that the two are contemporary. In view of the plan of the structures suggested by the earthwork platforms, the timber material and the relationship to the ridge and furrow, a mediaeval date could be suggested. It has all the appearance of a small agricultural set up, possibly a predecessor to the Wade house which lies further south to the east of Plumtree Banks Barn, complex B discussed below.

Earthwork Group B (Fig. 1)

There is little doubt that this group represents something structurally substantial. The top of the hill to the east of the barn has been considerably levelled and there are the remains of a considerable structure on the top. Ridge and furrow ploughing on the eastern half of these earthworks has probably levelled structures, as suggested by faint terraces now visible beneath the ploughing. The broad parallel terracing to the north, whose northern limits have been truncated by a modern canalized stream, has all the appearance of formal gardens. Taking into account the name of the stream immediately to the south, the Hall Gill, it is probable that this marks the site of the mansion of the Wade family, who are known to have had a hall on Plumtree Banks in the sixteenth and seventeenth centuries. Indeed the Pontefract doctor and antiquarian Nathaniel Johnstone visited *Plumtreebanks* on 31 July, 1669[1]. The building earthworks to the west of the barn are on a different alignment to the hall and garden earthworks to the east of the barn and may represent an earlier phase. Certainly the present track leading from Cocking Lane to Gate Croft is on its original, though narrower, line where it approaches the bridge over the Hall Gill but, north of the barn, it overlies earlier buildings. The similar alignment of this whole group of earthwork structures between the barn and the track, along with those under the track and to its north, suggests a similar plan alignment, which in itself suggests a number of phases, all of which pre-date the hall complex to the east of the barn.

The presence of the barn, amid a complex of earthworks representing earlier activity, is something that is becoming more and more familiar in the Dales. Barns in isolated positions within fields are often sited on archaeology. Whether dictated by an already levelled building site or a ready supply of building materials, or both, will only be revealed by future work.

Earthwork Group C (Fig. 1)

This group of successive hollow ways has already been discussed above. It suggests that the stretch of Cocking Lane, west of its intersection with Lumb Gill Lane, may be original when turnpiked in the eighteenth century, a suggestion supported by field route c coming down the hill from complex A and terminating on it. The sharp southerly turn of this sequence of routes, which then turn westwards to the hall site of complex B, suggests that the main interest of the Wades was northwards, both in terms of the main view of the house, its gardens and the direction from which they approached the house. The substantial depth to which the routes have been worn suggests considerable use over a long time. The deep hollow way (j) on the southern side of Cocking Lane, on the eastern side of the Hall Gill, may well mark the line of the Roman Road from Elslack to Ilkley. It is known further north-west as Street Lane but its course to Ilkley has not been traced with certainty.

Earthwork Group D (Fig. 2)

The group of earthworks in the valley of the Hall Gill and on its southern slopes represent a remarkably well preserved late mediaeval water-powered iron working complex. The water power is provided by the gill, the site so positioned to obtain the maximum power yet provide room for the buildings. The site lies at the mouth of the Hall Gill, where it broadens out into flatter ground. Such a site is typical of many other mediaeval iron working sites elsewhere in the Yorkshire Pennines, notably a recently surveyed extensive complex on the Back Gill and Kidstone Gill at the head of Bishopdale.

The dam (m) retained the main pond whose edges are clearly defined on the north by an intermittent line of boulder walling and by three depressions on the southern bank of the stream, possibly representing intermittent silting of the much larger pond. The heavily revetted platforms immediately north of the dam (n,o), on the eastern side of the stream, represent stone structures probably used for storing charcoal. The site of the furnace associated with this dam, as suggested by the slag heap, has not been identified but buildings in which a large and ready supply of the charcoal fuel were stored would be adjacent. The second dam, pond and building(s) (p,q,r,s) on the western bank probably represent a forge site. It is likely that the southern arm of the hollow access way to the hall complex has destroyed parts of the iron working complex. The small earthwork group on the southern slopes of the Hall Gill valley is clearly related to the iron working complex, as a terraced way (w) connects the two. It seems likely that this group represents the living quarters of the iron master who worked the site.

There is no direct internal evidence for dating the site. The absence of a number of phases in its life suggests a short period of activity. It has been suggested (p. 24) that the will of John Smythe als Waud, dated 1439, refers to the site. If that is the case, as seems likely, then the importance of the site increases. Not only is it a remarkably well preserved complex with both living and working elements but it appears to represent both the smelting and the forging process and can, in all probability, be dated to the middle years of the fifteenth century.

Discussion

This appendix has summarised the results of the survey and presented some interpretations. A fuller account will be published elsewhere. The earthwork survey is only the first step in understanding what is there. The site was visited at different times of day, strength of sun and shadow, different weather conditions and under varying growths of grass. Some parts of the site need further visits to gain a better understanding. It is hoped that various geophysical techniques will be used, particularly on the iron working complex, to reveal underground features. The likely close date for the iron making sites makes the waste slags from the smelting process of paramount importance. It is possible to date slags, as their compositions vary with time and slags from undated sites can be compared with dated ones.

This extensive and complicated historic site was previously unknown apart from the iron working area. Documentary work suggests a larger number of smaller fields in the sixteenth and seventeenth centuries than exist now. Even with hindsight they were not identified – even with the practised eye! The significance of the documentary evidence will be discussed in the proposed more detailed paper.

It is often assumed by the non-specialist that the publication of surveys is the end of the process. It is only the start of understanding and can lead to other disciplines such as documentary evidence and geophysical techniques adding information which can provide a much fuller picture.

Reference

1. Nathaniel and Henry Johnstone, note books. Bodleian Library, MS Top Yorks, C13/f51v (Oxford)

Acknowledgements

I would like to thank the two farmers on whose land the earthworks lay, Mr. Lloyd Wallbank of Gate Croft Farm and Mr. Neville Wallbank of Lumb Gill Farm. Without their consent the survey would not have been possible. Mrs. Kate Mason first drew my attention to the iron working site many years ago. Lastly my children, Christopher and Frances, helped on numerous occasions with the survey, while Christopher has helped to produce the two published figures.

Index

(Entries in italics refer to illustrations)

field systems and types, 27-30, *80*, 131, *132-3*,
  136-7; closes, enclosures, 28, 30, 79, 81,
  103-4; intakes, 28, 79, 113, 129; strips, 20,
  27, 29-30; *see also* open fields, ploughing,
  rig and furrow.
Fieldhouse family, 36, 77
Fir Cottage, 43, 45, 46, *48*, 60
Fleece Inn, 31, 43, 54, 56, 72
football, 100, 112
Fox George, 41
Frank, Elizabeth and Ingram, 45, 63, 64, 72
friendly societies, 93-4
Friends' Meeting House, *41*, 60, 123
fulling mill, 16, 18

Garlic, John, schoolmaster, 77
Gaskell, Mrs. Elizabeth, 92, 106
Gatecroft, 36, 39, 41, 94, 131, *132*; Upper,
  40, 44, *52*, 53, 60; Lower, 54, 55, *80*; *see also*
  Overgate Croft
Gildersber, *13*, 16, 45, 58, 60, 92; cottage at,
  54; lands at, 22-3, 24; name of (Thomas
  of), 17, 18, 23
Gill House, 75, *80*, 128
Goodrick, Henry, 40
Gray, Thomas, poet, 70, 83
Green (Greene) families, 18, 19, 35, 61, 73; of
  Low House, 45, 60, 77
Green, The, house at, 45, 54, 58, 60
Greenwood family, 77, 96, 128
Grimshaw, Rev. William, 76
Guyer family, 58, 76

Haghead, *13*, 14, 127, 129
Hall, The (earliest manor house), 14, 25, 43,
  130
Hall Crofts, or Hallcrofts (fields), 14, 20, *21*,
  27, 28, 130
Hallcroft Hall, 86, 109
Hall Orchard (later Church Orchard), 14, *21*,
  25, 27, 28
Hardcastle, Mary, 42
Hardwick family, 18, 19, 25
Hardwick (Holes) Farm, 25, *80*, 128
Hargreaves family, 60, 65, 83, 109
Harrison family (of The Green), 45, 58, 59,
  60, 79

Harrison, Stephen, 56, 57
Hart (Hard) Ridding, or Hutred (field), 22-3
Hartley family, 9, 34
Hartley, Bernard, surveyor, 72
Hawksworth, Sir Nicholas, 32
health and sickness, 34, 93; district nurse, 118;
  doctors, 91, 92, 105, 130.
hearth tax, 44-5, 81
Heathness, *21*, 28, 29
Heber, Reginald, 61
Heselhead, Heselwod (field), *13*, 22
Hewerdine, Harry, 102, 118
High Bank House, 55, 60, 85
High Field (Highfield), 12, *13*, 20, *21*; as
  arable land, 20, 28.
Highfield House, 55, 110
High House, Main Street, 60, 86, 88, 91
High House, Moorside, 54, 60, *80*
High Mill, 72-3, 83, 86, 88, 98, 105; *see also*
  cornmill.
High Moor, *80*, 81, 103-4
Hird, William and Ann, 41, *52*, 53, 60
Hodgson, Jane, 72
Hodson's Farm, *80*
Holdsworth, Thomas, 44
Holgate, William, 20
Hollin Hall, Ilkley, 20, 25, 44, 61
Holme House, 54, 55, 97
Holmes family, 19, 32, 35, 88, 95, 128;
  inventories for, 57, 58
Holmes, Hilda, *4, 41, 78, 87, 89*
Holmes, The (fields on low ground), 20, 22,
  130; Brereton Holme and Short Holme, *13*,
  21, 27; Wade Holme, 124, *126*
Horsfall, Jeremiah, 86, 95, 101
Horsman families, 100
houses, 43-56, 82, 105; timber-framed, 43-4,
  46, 134, 137; built or repaired for the poor,
  34-5, 36, 56, 100; *see also* names of
  individual houses, especially: Brockabank,
  Cragg House, Crossbank, Fir Cottage,
  Gatecroft, The Hall, Lumb Beck, Main
  Street, manor houses, Overgate Croft,
  Plumtree Banks, Rectory, Stamp Hill,
  Street House Farm.
Hunger Hill, *21*, 28
Hustwick, William, 65

Round Dykes, *2*, 3, 104
Rushforth, Alice, 34

Sailor Inn, 44, 72, 110
Sandbeds, Sandylands (field), *15*, 27, 29, 40, 111, 127
Sanfitt, Low Sanfitt, 45, 53, 60
sawmill, 45, 60, 97, 111, 116; *see also* Fentiman's Mill
Saxey, William, 20
Scalegill, *13*, 22
Scargill Farm, 75, 76, *80*
schools, 77-9, 93, 100-3, 118-120
School Wood (farm), 28, 44, 54, *80*
Seed, James, 96
Shackleton family, 59, 60
Shaw, John, 67
sheep, 58, 79, 100, 114
Shipton, William, 90
Shires family, 34, 37
shops and tradesmen, 91, 105, 112, 113
Short Holme, 27
Silsden, 30, 31, 61, 76, 103-4, 129; disputed boundary with, 74-5, 104, 128.
Silsden Moor, 3, 74, 75, 76
Simon the Smith, 17, 22, 24
Simpson, Sidney, 119
Skipton, 1, 23, 30-3, 55, 62, 64; schools in, 23, 28, 77, 118, 119; roads to, 30, 39, 69, 70, 71, 129; railway to, 96, 107-9, 111; Poor Law Union, 91; Rural District Council, 105, 108, 111, 121, 123; *see also* Ermysted's School, Skipton Castle.
Skipton Castle, 6, 31, 32-3, 37, 75, 125; Romille and Clifford families at, 12, 16; siege of, 32-3.
Slade Farm, 73, 75, *80*
Slater, John, 103
Small Banks, 45, 46, *47*, 54, 59, 60
Smith, Richard, 18th-century Lord of the Manor, 60, 83, 84, 94; family of, 42, 62, 64, 94, 105; diary of, 91-2; millstone quarry and, 73, 74, 75; defining boundaries, 125, 127.
Smith, Robert, housewright, 43
Smith, Stephen, 42
Smith, William, manufacturer, 96

Smithy Greaves, *13*, 23-4, 29, 40, 70, 83, 130
Smyth, John (alias Waud), 24, 138
Southfield (Suffield), 16, 20, *21*, 28
Spencer families, 34, 64, 72, 79, 103, 109; masons and quarrymen, 64, 65, 74.
Spencer's Gill, 109
Speight, Harry, 64
spinning, 73, 76, 83, 86-8
Springfield Mount, 111
Springs (field), 22
Stamp Hill, house at, 36, 100, 117
Steel Sidney, 113
Stott, William and Ellen, 33, 57, 72
Street or Bullcommon, 16, *21*, 29, *126*; as former Roman road, 3, *38*, 39, 138
Street Farm, Stockinger Lane, 53
Street House Farm, 30, 54, 60, 92
Stubbings (field), 22
Sunbank Farm, 54, *80*
Swan Inn, 100
Swire, Samuel, map by, 90

Tadcaster, 3, 14, 32, 66, 69
Taylor, Ellen, 44
Teal, Hugh, 128-9
Teale, John, 67, 74
Tenant, John, 42
textile industry, 86-90, 97-8, 115-116; fulling mills, 16, 18; domestic production, 19, 55, 82-3, 87; wool and worsted, 58, 73, 79, 82-3, 86; cotton, linen, silk, 82, 86, 97-8, 115; spinning mills, 73, 77, 86-8; children employed in, 86, 93.
Thack Wood Ing (field), 20, *21*, 27
Thanet, Earl of, 36-7, 81
Thompson, Elizabeth, 34
Thompson, William, 62, 63, 64-5, 101; family of, 83, 85
Thompson-Ashby family, 63
Threlfall, William, 96, 97, 101
Tison, Gislebert, 11, 12
tithes, tithe-map, 30, 64, *80*, 96
Toller, Peter, 23, 26, 28
Topham, Thomas, 60
Tophan, John, 36
Townend (Town End), 20, 43
Town Gate, 20